PREDATORS IN OUR PULPITS

PREDATORS IN OUR PULPITS

W. Phillip Keller

HARVEST HOUSE PUBLISHERS
Eugene, Oregon 97402

Except where otherwise indicated, Scripture quotations in this book are taken from the King James Version of the Bible.

PREDATORS IN OUR PULPITS

Copyright © 1988 by Harvest House Publishers
Eugene, Oregon 97402

Library of Congress Cataloging-in-Publication Data

Keller, W. Phillip (Weldon Phillip), 1920-
    Predators in our pulpits.

        1. Christian life—1960-   2. Christian
leadership.   I. Title.
BV4501.2.K4255   1988   262'.1   87-83692
ISBN 0-89081-674-3

Printed in the United States of America.

By the Same Author

Splendor from the Sea
As a Tree Grows
Bold Under God—A Fond Look at a Frontier Preacher
A Shepherd Looks at Psalm 23
A Layman Looks at the Lord's Prayer
Rabboni—Which Is to Say, Master
A Shepherd Looks at the Good Shepherd and His Sheep
A Gardener Looks at the Fruits of the Spirit
Mighty Man of Valor—Gideon
Mountain Splendor
Taming Tension
Expendable
Still Waters
A Child Looks at Psalm 23
Ocean Glory
Walking with God
On Wilderness Trails
Elijah—Prophet of Power
Salt for Society
A Layman Looks at the Lamb of God
Lessons from a Sheep Dog
Wonder o' the Wind
Joshua—Man of Fearless Faith
A Layman Looks at the Love of God
Sea Edge
Chosen Vessels
David I
David II
Sky Edge

In Appreciation

First of all genuine gratitude is given to my Father in Heaven for the courage, strength, and fortitude to complete this work He has given me to do.

Secondly, my sincere appreciation goes to Ursula, my wife, who not only typed the manuscript with care, but also listened quietly to each chapter as it was read to her.

Thirdly, a special note of thanks is given to the many lay people who not only urged me to write this book but also undertook to pray for the project.

Contents

The Peril

The Peril

This little book is an earnest word of warning addressed to the children of God worldwide. It comes from a common man to the common people in all sorts of groups and congregations scattered everywhere across the earth.

Its theme and thrust is not new or novel. There have always been *false prophets* among those who posed as leaders for God's people. From ancient times God has cried out against the so-called *under-shepherds* who plundered and ravaged His people.

Always, in every generation, there have been insidious imposters who, pretending to be true shepherds, were in fact predators in disguise. In cunning craftiness they have posed as legitimate leaders, while at the same time tearing to pieces God's little flock.

The true prophets of old cried out against their predation upon God's sheep. (See Ezekiel 34.)

Our Lord Jesus Christ warned His contemporaries of their depredation. (See Matthew 7:15 and chapter 23.)

The apostles of the early church were alert to this enormous peril among their people. (See 1 and 2 Timothy.)

TODAY THERE ARE PREDATORS
IN OUR PULPITS!

The greatest threat to the church of Jesus Christ in the world today is not from without, as so many suppose, but rather from its own leadership within. Our greatest danger of destruction is not from outside forces arrayed against Christians, but from the counterfeits who mislead their followers within the flock. We are being preyed upon and know it not.

Because of the rather unique and unusual pattern of my own spiritual saga, which exposed me to the work of God throughout the world in a wide variety of denominations, I have seen this peril firsthand. The tardiness with which I was delayed in committing my life fully to Christ was in part because of the false teaching received from some of the leaders who preyed on my searching soul. My spirit hungered and thirsted for God with burning intensity. Yet more often than not the men in the pulpit led me only to empty stalls and dry, broken cisterns.

What was true for me has likewise been the tragic story of millions of other earnest, seeking people in the pews. And now as I enter the twilight years of my life, there has been laid upon me a burden of intercessory prayer for leaders everywhere within the church. Increasingly one salient conviction becomes clear by the instruction of God's Spirit: IF THERE IS TO BE SPIRITUAL AWAKENING IN THE PEW, IT MUST FIRST BEGIN IN THE PULPIT!

For a number of years now there has been a growing inner compulsion to cry out to my own generation about this peril in our pulpits. Very often when the concern was shared with others, the response has been less than encouraging. Some have stated rather bluntly that such a note of alarm is too negative, too disturbing, perhaps even too divisive.

None of these is intended; quite the opposite. This little book is written to alert God's people, to call them to action, to awaken them before they are consumed.

It should be pointed out here that this book is essentially a plea to lay people from an ordinary layman. It is written in layman's language so that the average person in the pew can grasp its message with clarity. It makes no pretense at being a profound, scholarly work. It is not intended to intimidate professional clergymen, some of whom are bound to read it. But it is hoped that they will be honest enough to examine their own motives and messages in the light of its themes.

It would be very much easier not to pen these lines, for it has been well stated:

> Prophets are praised when they are dead, but they are persecuted while they are alive.

In view of this I do have a single, simple request to make of the reader, no matter who it may be: Please do not write me letters either of appreciation or of abuse for what is written here. This work is not intended to arouse conflict or controversy. It is commissioned, rather, by God's Spirit for men and women to examine their own lives and the life of their Christian group before God.

In this connection a brief comment needs to be made about the phrase "predators in our pulpits." Modern-day pulpits take many forms. They are much more than just the podium in a church sanctuary. There are television programs, radio broadcasts, publishing houses, printing presses, home Bible study groups, church retreats, campgrounds, evangelistic campaigns, and other church-related activities. In scores of ways and in thousands of different places all sorts of people are provided with a platform or "pulpit" from which to promulgate their ideas and exert their leadership.

No matter how far-ranging their influence or how small their following, always the question which must be asked is: "Are these leaders authentic under-shepherds, or are they predators preying on people?"

Of course many common people really have no way of knowing. In their trusting simplicity they are being led astray by the very teachers whom they assume are instructing them in truth. The laity look to them for life while being led to the slaughter, or at least to impotence.

The stark truth is that multitudes are being deluded to believe a lie. They are being deceived by the very ones they thought had only their best interests in mind. There has been an insidious infiltration of the church by men and women whose work and words spell its destruction.

In spite of all the grandiose claims made in recent years about the condition of the church worldwide, the fact remains that God's people are in reality still only a "little flock." Our Lord stated categorically that there would be few who would find His way or follow faithfully in His footsteps.

It has always been so.

A part of the reason that so many stumble down the broad road to destruction is simply that they have been led there by false teachers and perilous preachers. Perhaps by reading this book with an open mind and sensitive spirit some will be spared from that terrible end.

For my part, this message goes out to my generation with the earnest prayer that our Father will use it to preserve His people amid their peril in these darkening days.

This book has two distinct parts to it. The first half serves as a simple guide by which an ordinary layperson can determine to some degree whether or not his or her spiritual leader is in truth one of those people called of God to be an under-shepherd to Christ.

Part I helps common people to put spiritual values into a proper perspective from God's viewpoint. If read carefully, it is bound to raise some hard questions about leadership among Christians. It is intended to provide clear guidelines by which the actions and ministry of leaders may be assessed.

The second half of the book provides the very basic demands made by the Master upon anyone who may wish to follow Him. Part II is a very simple, categorical statement of what it costs to be a Christian in our contemporary society. This aspect of the Christian's life is scarcely mentioned today in the church, simply because most ministers are afraid it will alienate their people and diminish their following.

Contrary to what most might consider a negative emphasis, this is in truth a most positive appeal for a lofty life of loyalty and love for Christ. It is a clarion call for total commitment to His majesty, the Lord Jesus Christ.

Many false teachers and profane prophets are abroad in our culture. Christ warned us emphatically that this would be the case. Read carefully Matthew 24:4,5,24-26.

The purpose of the pages that follow is to warn God's people against some of those who would destroy them. We live in an affluent age of great danger. Only as we are alert can we avert the wiles of those who would prey upon us.

PREDATORS IN OUR PULPITS

Part I

THE ROLE OF THE LEADER: HIS HIGH CALLING UNDER GOD

Beware of the false teachers—men who come to you in sheep's fleece, but beneath that disguise they are ravenous wolves.
—Jesus Christ
in Matthew 7:15 (Weymouth)

It is the half-Christian clergy, of every denomination, that are the main cause of the so-called failure of the Church of Christ.

—George MacDonald

1

The Lure
of
Leadership

In human society most people want to be led.

The majority of mankind prefer to let others make the hard decisions for them.

Most people choose the easy path of simply accepting what others in positions of authority tell them.

To use Biblical language, human beings are like sheep with the "mob instinct" that impels them to follow any Pied Piper. As long as he plays a pleasant tune they will submit themselves to his will and fall prey to his wishes.

The reverse side of this odd behavior in human society is the sobering fact that a few among us find enormous attraction in the role of leadership. It is the path to power, to prestige, and to personal prominence. This is true whether it be in politics, business, education, athletics, or religion. In every area of human activity there can be found an arena of self-aggrandizement for the one eager to lead.

Therein lies the great peril.

Few common people seem to realize how quickly an ambitious individual can come to power. They seem baffled by the meteoric rise of aggressive persons to positions of prominence. They are often totally dazzled by the display and are ultimately deluded by the self-indulgence of the leader—unless of course it be an unusual person of great benevolence. Such are rare indeed.

The net result is that in many instances the leader, instead of serving others in humility, is in truth serving his or her own interests. In vivid contrast to this, Christ Himself stated clearly, "The Son of man came not to be ministered unto but to minister [serve], and to give His life a ransom for many." Read carefully Matthew 20:20-28.

Our Lord was even more forthright about this matter when He stated dramatically, "Whosoever will be chief among you, let him be your servant." This was a difficult concept for His followers to grasp in a society where greatness was always equated with power, greed, prestige, and great personal gain.

Across the centuries since Christ came among us in human form as a servant, men and women of all creeds have had to examine their motives for ministry in the light of His humility and utter self-denial. Why do they serve at all?

The hard and searching question which must be asked of anyone in Christian leadership is: "Why are you in this role? Is it for personal advancement, or is it to please God and bring benefit to others?" It demands enormous inner integrity to answer this question with open honesty.

The clear and uncluttered answer will quickly help to decide whether the leader is indeed one called of Christ to be an under-shepherd to His people or is merely a charlatan. The laypeople in any group are fully entitled to know the underlying motives which have moved their leaders into positions of prominence. They should not be afraid to ask the hard question, "Are you called to this role by our Father God, or have you chosen it for purely personal reasons of self-gratification?"

The second serious aspect of this matter is that laypeople tend to put their pastors on a pedestal. Simply because an individual places himself or herself in a position of prominence, he or she is often treated with an aura of adulation not deserved.

It is one thing for a person to know assuredly that he has been set apart for service to the Most High, to know that he has been sent with a message from the Lord for His people, to know that it is the Word of God, under the unction of God the Holy Spirit, which will draw wayward men and women to Christ. It is quite another matter to merely take up a pastoral role as a convenient career that panders to one's own personal tastes or ambitions.

The distinction between these two roles is to be measured not in the numbers of those who may or may not be influenced by the speaker. Rather, the difference lies in whether the message delivered is indeed from God and bears the ring of truth and the stamp of His approval.

In ancient times if the word of the prophet did not come to pass he was put to death for his deceit. In our soft society today almost any charlatan can attract a crowd and be applauded for his or her popularity no matter how corrupt the pronouncements may be.

There are two important criteria by which the true man of God may be discerned. The first is that his message is in keeping with the Scripture and not contrary to the clear commands of Christ. The second is that he comes to his people with great humility of heart and sensitivity to the guidance of God's gracious Spirit. He does not promulgate his own personal views nor parade himself with an aura of prestige or power.

If there is to be a demonstration of power among God's people it should not pander to the personal vanity and pride of the leader. The Word of God itself is spirit and is truth. Christ Himself is that Word incarnate. It is He who redeems us, justifies us, recreates us, enlivens us with His own presence, and calls us His own. To Him all honor is due!

There is another serious aspect to Christian service not clearly understood by the common people, and that is the whole matter of accountability. If indeed the leader is a genuine man or woman of God, he will have a keen sense of dual responsibility both to the Lord and to those whom he has been called to serve.

The Scriptures make it very clear that the three main duties of an under-shepherd are to feed the flock with spiritual sustenance, to pray for them in compassion and loving concern, and to rescue the lost and wandering ones, protecting them from falling prey to predators.

To carry out these responsibilities properly demands a very high degree of daily self-discipline. Time simply must be set apart to commune with Christ, to meditate over His Word, to receive a message directly from the Father above for His people on earth. Unless the leader has been touched with truth in his own spirit, it is most unlikely that his message can ever inspire, uplift, or enlighten others in eternal ways that endure.

Precisely the same principle applies to private prayer. If our Lord, when He was on earth, found it imperative to spend hours alone in prayer with His Father, how much more should this be true of our human leaders! They must be those who know God, who enjoy His intimacy, who can call on Him with calm confidence at any time.

These activities are much more important than any other in which the minister may engage. There is no substitute for them. It takes time, much time alone with God, in order to serve His people well. The tragic truth is that some leaders in our pulpits do not do this because no one supervises their private lives.

The high calling to which God calls those chosen ones to speak on His behalf is not only a holy duty but also a lonely life. It is to be very much among the suffering and sorrows of our society but also (more often than not) somewhat alone in bearing the burdens—frequently misunderstood and often wrongly accused. Christ came to us as the Man of Sorrows, acquainted with grief. So it is to be expected that those who follow Him will taste the same suffering and endure the same disdain.

This is inevitable. It is a part of the high cost that anyone is called to pay if he is to have a great compassion for the lost and perishing. It is no easy thing to gather up the wayward and willful wanderers of the world. It is heart-wrenching work that strains the soul, wearies the body, and crushes the spirit. Yet there is no other way in which those called of Christ can become "broken bread" or "poured-out wine" to a perishing people, in which a few hunger and thirst for God Himself.

To devote one's self to such a labor of love demands much more than mere human sympathy for suffering people. To dedicate one's whole life and energy to the children of men calls for much more than compassion. Such consecration can only be sustained by undivided devotion to Christ Himself. For He, and only He, can possibly supply the resources required to remedy the wrongs in our weary old world.

The person in a position of leadership, no matter how prominent or how obscure, must be one whose very life is grounded in God Himself. The energy and vitality and love to reach the lost must come from Christ resident within that individual. Any action taken and any decisions made should be under the clear direction of God's Spirit.

It simply will not do to use one's own charm, talents, or elaborate techniques to try to accomplish God's work in the world. And so laypeople are entitled to see the very life of Christ in their leaders.

Positive proof that the one in the pulpit is sent of God lies not only in his humility, compassion, and communion with Christ, but also in the calm courage of his character. The leader must be one who is utterly fearless for God, not in an overbearing or dictatorial manner, but rather in relentless loyalty and love to the Master.

This person will not pander to the selfish interests of his hearers. He will not accommodate his message to the corruption of his culture. He will be above petty politics among his congregation. He will stand solid for the truth revealed to him in God's Word. He will not dilute or diminish the noble demands made by God for His called-out people. Nor will he hesitate to confront the wrongs in his community without flinching.

The above is no easy assignment. It calls for enormous faith in God as well as great fortitude in personal conduct. At times it may make one exceedingly unpopular with certain elements in society. But this should be so. If the truth is proclaimed with the unction of God's gracious Spirit, it is bound to polarize people. Christ Himself stated categorically, *"Either you are for me or you are against me."*

The people in the pews are entitled to look for unflinching faithfulness to God and to His Word in the life and language of their leaders. If they are to follow with surety, then they must be led with steadfast courage and vision.

The minister's role is not to make people comfortable in their padded pews. He is not there to pander to the petty preferences of his parishioners. He is there to proclaim the whole counsel of God. He is there to declare eternal truth. He is there to call men and women to Christ.

Far too many contemporary Christian churches and mission organizations do not seek for such leadership. Instead, they place undue importance upon personal charm, eloquent speech, academic credentials, or organizational ability. It is almost as if they were advertising for a business executive to run a commercial corporation rather than searching for God's spokesman. Little wonder that they frequently end up with predators in their pulpits!

The end result may well be a slick and smooth success by worldly standards, but this does not mean that the great purposes of God for His people have been achieved. Often all that is accomplished is the consolidation of another social club where people come for food, fun, and fellowship. God's work in the world is not advanced, but the people are deluded to believe the opposite. They are deceived and know it not.

A genuine man of God does not even try to come to an easy accommodation with our decadent society. At great personal cost and at the risk of being very unpopular he will dare to be "a voice in the wilderness," the prophet of his generation calling people to repentance. He will seek the lost sunk in sin. He will warn them to turn from their wicked ways. He will go out with tears and come in with gladness, bringing some who were astray home to the Master.

Such a leader is not intimidated by his contemporaries. He is called of God to noble service, and he does not draw back from his duties. His people cannot muzzle him. The world cannot silence his message. And the enemy trembles, for he is a man of truth. He does not hesitate to challenge others to follow Christ at any cost. Nor does he delude them into the false belief that it is easy to be the Master's man. He will urge his fellow pilgrims to count the cost of following Christ. He will enable them to see what a glorious honor it is to be a child of the Most High.

2

The Success Syndrome

The Western world is completely convinced that there is absolutely no substitute for success. This intense preoccupation with success impinges upon every part of Western society, including the church. Success is really just a synonym for the "biggest," "brightest," and "best," whatever that may mean.

Such "success" is not necessarily measured in terms of quality, purity, honesty, or even sincerity. Rather, it is closely associated with the idea of whatever is spectacular, sensational, and striking to our senses. Westerners are captivated by showmanship. They are mesmerized by that which panders to human pride or feeds human vanity.

This vain view of life is inculcated in our children

from their earliest years. Our entire educational system instructs young people to "shoot for the top," to "go for the limit," to "make a big splash," to "make a million." This success syndrome is further nourished by the entire entertainment world, where all sorts of theatrics, camouflage, and brazen showmanship are used to exalt superficial "stars." If we don't have genuine heroes, we set out to fabricate them in the minds of a gullible public.

In business, commerce, education, athletics, and even the arts, every effort is made to so exalt either an individual or an enterprise that it appears to be a success. We even have a favorite saying which sums it all up: "There is no success like success!"

So long and so persistently has this concept been an integral part of Western culture that our people accept it as the proper and appropriate way to go. It is regarded as a mark of success if a church is growing rapidly in numbers even though most of its members may have no deep commitment to Christ. It is considered a success if a pastor can sway his people with nothing more than showmanship.

Again and again in the contemporary church we discover that the main preoccupation, not only of the pastor but also of the people, is the so-called "program." The basic idea is to provide something so sensational and appealing that it attracts crowds and stimulates a substantial increase in attendance. If this is happening, then human vanity is gratified and our deep desire to impress people with our so-called "success" is somehow satisfied.

This is true of every area of Christian enterprise— not just the local church in the home village, town, or city. It applies equally to the leaders and their close associates in the electronic church; in evangelism; in publishing; in institutional endeavors. The same old tarnished techniques of attracting a following and impressing the public are used. The wretched, weary old ways of the world are employed to try to pack in the people.

All sorts of courses are offered in "church growth." Seminars are held all over the country on "human dynamics," instructing would-be leaders in how to attract crowds. Books are written on the theme. Even the most blatant and brazen styles of communication spawned in Hollywood and Nashville are employed to appeal to the masses. Almost any means is considered valid and acceptable as long as it produces the end result of gathering a crowd. Success is the ultimate criterion measured in mass attendance, even if the true final results are miniscule.

This injection of the world's view of success into the life of the twentieth-century church has captured the imagination of its leaders. The consequence is that in many instances the basic claims offered to us by Christ are completely ignored or not understood at all.

It is strange indeed that He invariably spoke of His own followers as being few in number. He made it very clear that most people would never walk in His paths. The challenge was too great, the demands of self-denial too tough, the call to total loyalty and love for Him too lofty.

Yet our religious leaders keep boasting about a "moral majority" or "worldwide awakenings" or "mass evangelism" or "ecumenical unity." If indeed these be valid, why does the whole complexion of our contemporary society not change? Why do not 55 million so-called Christians in North America make it one of the truly righteous regions of the earth instead of one of the most corrupt? Why is it that today, percentage-wise, there are fewer true followers of Christ on the earth than in the past hundred years?

The basic fact is that the majority of Christians really have been deceived. The preoccupation of our leaders, in whatever public pulpit they occupy, in most cases has been to try to impress the public with their success. There are two bedrock reasons for this. The first is that they dare not appear to be a failure. The second is that their continuing support, whether moral, social, or financial, depends upon being considered a success. In our culture ordinary people simply do not back a loser.

So it follows that the leader must of necessity always appear to be successful. He must be on the move. His enterprise must be growing in size and scale. He must be making an impact on the masses. If he does not, he is doomed to sure defeat.

All of this stands in sharp and stunning contrast to the life of our Lord. He made no concerted attempt to amuse, entertain, or attract crowds. When they did gather round Him, He simply met their basic needs for hunger, healing, and help. He never tried to impress anyone.

The Master never tried to manipulate the multitudes. He looked upon them as lost sheep gone astray. (See Matthew 9:35-38.) He saw Himself as the great Good Shepherd who could help them in their extremity. He spoke simple truth to them which often dismayed those who wished to be His disciples. He restored health to those who were ill. He freed those held captive by evil forces. He fed the hungry which came to Him. In the midst of all this service, never once did He capitalize on His popularity or attempt to use public acclaim to establish a great sphere of influence for Himself. He refused adamantly to establish any sort of earthly empire among His admirers.

All of this stands in startling juxtaposition to contemporary church leaders, who so often use every means possible to build a little kingdom around themselves. Many of them pander to the public in order to promote their own personalities and to advance their own ambitions for glory or gain.

If this cannot be achieved by means of numerical church growth, then a second common strategy is for the leader to plunge his people into a vigorous building program. The sheer excitement of erecting new buildings of ornate design is a slick strategy for involving all the adherents. People will gladly participate in pouring concrete, nailing studs, or contributing generously to the construction of an impressive new sanctuary that panders to their own personal prestige in the community.

Some pastors spend the greater part of their time, energy, and lives in simply erecting monuments of brick, stone, glass, and timber to their own genius. Beautiful buildings are supposedly a mark of success in spiritual matters. Jesus looked at the temple and told His followers that it would be torn down to the ground. And it was! *It had been turned into a den of thieves.*

The end result of all such activities is that in many instances the church takes on the complexion of a common commercial enterprise. The main thrust is to set up elaborate human machinery to maintain its momentum, thus deluding people into believing that really great things are being accomplished for God. Yet in very truth these same sanctuaries are but ornate mausoleums where the dead bury the dead.

All over the Western world, including Europe and its satellite countries, thousands of churches stand almost silent. Moss grows deep on their roofs and walls. Spiders spin their webs over the stained-glass windows, while the pews are empty but for a mere handful of elderly adherents who came there hoping against hope to hear a word from on high.

The ordinary people of the community will not come to the church except to be married or to be buried. It is their implicit conviction that it is but another commercial venture in society. They believe, sometimes with good grounds, that all the pastor or minister is interested in is their contributions in cash. They look on religion as a money-making scheme. So they simply stay away. Nor can they be blamed, for their deep human intuitions are perfectly valid. The church does nothing substantial to fill the great aching void in their spirits—the deep inner ache for God Himself. Yet unashamedly it plunders their pockets. Little wonder it is so often held in deep contempt!

Jesus, too, spoke out vehemently against the entrenched ecclesiastical exploitation of His times. He had the most scathing accusations for the religious leaders of His day who preyed upon the poor while lining their own pockets. His denunciations of the scribes, Pharisees, and hypocrites read like the most violent of revolutionary declarations. (See Matthew 23:1-39.)

Not only did Christ take issue with the entrenched religious leaders of His generation, but also with the basic behavior demonstrated within the spiritual life of the synagogues. In those days, as in ours, there was an ongoing duplicity that showed special partiality to the rich and prominent people while at the same time neglecting or abusing the poor and downtrodden.

The Success
Syndrome

To put it another way, society 2000 years ago was just as caught up with the "success syndrome" as it is in the late twentieth century. The priests, the scribes, the Pharisees—all the hypocritical leaders of the law catered to men and women of wealth, prominence, or popularity. These were given the place of prestige in the assemblies. They were treated with special adulation and approval. They were shown unusual deference in the deliberations of the synagogues.

Our Lord spoke out against this sort of thing with great fervor. So too did the apostles in their letters to the early church. For example, read James chapter 2 and chapter 5. The laypeople were warned that the wealthy ones would exploit them unduly if allowed to do so. All of this may seem to us in our democratic societies to be a bit outdated . . . but is it?

The astonishing fact is that identical attitudes still persist among the clergy. Few indeed are the ministers among us who have sufficient courage to confront the "successful" people in their congregations with absolute truth about their behavior. Where are the leaders with sufficient spiritual fortitude to demand of all their people the high standards of stewardship to which Christ calls us? Why do so-called Christian leaders so often remain silent about the matter of money and wealth and assets which their people should share with the poor and the needy?

A great many pastors or preachers are intimidated by the "successful" people, the brilliant business executives, and the popular social set who come to their churches. They try to cater to these social climbers by putting them into positions of prominence in the church hierarchy. They are given undue recognition in offices which demand weighty decisions. They are chosen for their personal charm, charisma, or status in the community rather than for their undeviating devotion to Christ.

Are we surprised then when the church becomes just another social club? Do we wonder why petty politics and why rivalry over power and influence play such a large part in the life of parishioners? Do we marvel that the man in the pulpit is made to be a mouse who dares not speak anything but sweet niceties to his congregation?

Because he is not brave enough to speak the whole truth on behalf of the Living God, lest his successful people silence him, he betrays all of them. He is faithful to neither his Father in heaven above nor to his earth children in the world below. The latter look to him for bread, spiritual bread, but instead they are given a sop that satisfies no one. His messages are trimmed to accommodate the private preferences of the successful people. He is sure that this is the only way he himself can be a success. Yet all the time he is betraying the trust given him by God.

The final consequence is that no one benefits. The one in the pulpit, who should have led his people onto the higher ground of walking with Christ in obedience to His Word, has actually dragged them down into the ditch of despair and cynicism. Inwardly they have nothing but contempt for the church, so they laugh at its leaders. Like so much in secular life, they know full well that it is all rather phony and a hollow mockery.

3

Misplaced
Faith

It follows that if the main preoccupation of any
Christian is sheer size of activity with its attendant
success measured in growth of members, the means
to that end will be largely of human design and ar-
rangement. There are, of course, some exceptions to this
principle. When people are led to genuine repentance
before the Lord, when under the conviction of God's
Spirit a community of Christians comes to turn from
its wicked ways, when in profound penitence people
pray for forgiveness from wrongdoing and cast themselves on Christ's mercy, then it is startling how many
men and women are brought into the family of God.

This essentially is the sovereign work of God our
Father. It does not depend on some special human

endeavor. Nor is it accomplished by the clever techniques of those who are taught how to manipulate the masses. Nor does it happen simply because laypeople have been taught how to bring others to the Master through some sort of specialized approach. It is at heart the lovely work of God's own gracious Spirit, who through various remarkable means brings a soul from darkness into the light of God's own truth; who lifts the human spirit from despair into Christ's love; who brings the lost from death into abundant life in God.

The reason such transformation does not take place more often is simply that our spiritual leaders mislead people in the exercise of their faith. The common man is induced to believe that he should invest his faith in some sort of creed, doctrine, or body of belief. He is sometimes persuaded that he should place his total confidence in "the church"—whatever that very broad, all-encompassing term may imply. And, of course, all too often the individual is encouraged to place his complete trust in the pastor, minister, speaker, or teacher who has touched his life.

It is precisely at any one of these three points that a person may easily fall prey to the most pernicious sort of propaganda. Even though the layperson may respond with the best of intentions to whatever he or she may be told, if it is falsehood the consequences can be utterly devastating. This does not apply merely to the so-called cults which proliferate on every side; it applies also to those established churches in which the leaders really do not love Christ or know Him in person.

The terrible fallout from such delusion has no doubt been more damaging to God's work and His wishes in the Western world than any other single factor. There are in truth literally millions of men and women in our sophisticated society who are totally turned off to Christianity. At some stage of their past spiritual experience they had put their faith, as best they knew how, into either a creed, a church congregation, or a clergyman—only to be deluded and double-crossed.

The creed did not provide the dynamic needed to live in a world of enormous stress and strain. The congregation, its members, or its social function may have been so selfish, so uncaring, so superficial that it alienated the adherent with its sham. The leader may have been less than a saint, a person with feet of clay who severely disappointed the new convert by his personal behavior.

Any one of these influences or all of them together might have been enough to drive the would-be follower to despise Christianity. This happens in thousands upon thousands of lives. What is the real problem? It is a matter of misplaced faith. And our leaders are responsible. A person should be led to invest his total trust not in the creed, not in the congregation, not in the clergy, but only in Christ Himself!

He is the only perfect One, who will never, never disappoint anyone who puts his or her implicit confidence in Him. The church across the centuries has frequently failed its people. Christ has never once failed the person who will trust Him in quiet faith and obedient love. I have written a number of books explaining to laypeople how this is done. Among them perhaps the most helpful are *A Shepherd Looks at Psalm 23, A Layman Looks at the Lord's Prayer, Walking With God,* and *Rabboni—Which Is to Say, Master.*

Any spiritual leader, no matter what arena of spiritual activity he or she operates in, has a most solemn and serious obligation to lead laypeople to Jesus Christ, the Living Lord, who is alive and active in the affairs of the earth and of our own personal lives. It is absolutely imperative that they should bring people to Him. It is essential that they be made to understand clearly what it has cost Christ to bring us His own wondrous life. That cost is His own perfect life among us, His own perfect sacrifice in our stead, His perfect death to atone for our sins, His glorious and marvelous resurrection to assure us of His divine power and living reality, His majestic ascension to the position of power where He intercedes and cares for us as His own, His gracious and generous bestowal of His own Holy Spirit to quicken and enliven us with His own eternal and supernatural life by His residence within us, and the wondrous assurance that now our Father enfolds us with endless compassion in His family.

Out of enormous gratitude for such generosity, our leaders should encourage us to invest our total faith and utter trust in Christ. They should call us to accept the challenge gladly to deny ourselves daily in order to follow Christ with good cheer at any cost. They should inspire us to be disciples who will demonstrate profound loyalty and deep love to Christ by quietly carrying out His commands in wholehearted goodwill.

As the Apostle John first put it so well: "We love Him because He first loved us!" (1 John 4:19). And this love of which he speaks is much, much more than some spurious, soft, sentimental emotion. Rather, it is the strong, powerful, dedicated determination of the will to serve God and to lay down our lives in order to benefit others. This is our faith in God finding fulfillment and fruition in doing good deeds for the benefit and blessing of others . . . not for our own selfish self-interests.

Again here, many contemporary Christian leaders are actually deceiving their followers. They are openly and without shame advocating the use of faith as a means of personal gain and self-advancement. It is a false emphasis which appeals dramatically to the inherent ego and perverse pride of unregenerate man. No wonder their churches are crammed with crowds! Little marvel their media outreach attracts the multitudes! It is no surprise that they can claim to be reaching the whole world with such great good news. Who wouldn't want to hear that it was his legitimate right to demand health and wealth as well as leisure and pleasure from God and to expect immediate delivery of same?

This spurious sort of contemporary teaching has swept over the entire earth. Its message has been expedited by the use of books, pamphlets, cassettes, radio broadcasts, television programs, and charismatic preachers and teachers in all sorts of pulpits. They use weekend retreats, special seminars, evangelistic crusades, and any other human agency to excite and arouse their audiences.

Always the emphasis is: "Expect your miracle from God"; "profess whatever you want, then possess it"; "insist on your right to health and wealth"; "look for signs and wonders"—all to serve your own desires. Seldom is the question asked: "O God in Christ, what can I do to serve You and Your people?"

In both 2 Corinthians chapter 11 and 2 Thessalonians chapter 2 the Spirit of God, speaking to the church through the Apostle Paul, warns of this sort of enticing and deceptive subversion. It would be used to distract Christ's followers from the simplicity of the

Gospel as it had been revealed in the accomplished work of Christ.

The teaching that puts such enormous emphasis on power, miracles, signs, and wonders holds enormous fascination for the modern mind. Like the success syndrome, it bears within it all that is sensational, spectacular, or startling. It appeals to the senses and leads people to believe that such signs, even if counterfeited, are indicative of profound spirituality or a special awareness of God.

Those caught up with such demonstrations of their faith in action are seldom aware of why they are actually in antagonism to the eternal purposes of The Most High. Stated most simply, it is this: God will not get His honor from nor share His splendor with mere men or women who claim His power to promote their own selfish ends. He will not allow Himself to become a mere tool in the hands of power-hungry people. This applies both to leaders and laity. Quite the opposite! His desire is that we human beings be made the instruments of His service to the wretched world in which we live.

So it must be asked in all sincerity and honesty: "Why do you wish to be healed?" "Why do you want to be made well?" "Why should you enjoy buoyant health?" All the simple, pat answers given to these searching questions will not suffice if we are going to be Christians of integrity. Is it simply so we are set free from suffering? Is it so we can boast about our faith healing? Is it just so we can be comfortable and coast along easily through life?

Or is health a gift granted so we can serve God better?

There is no question whatever that God our Father is deeply concerned about every detail of our lives.

42

Jesus the Christ alerted us to the simple, stirring truth that even the number of hairs on our heads is known. He cared when even a fledgling sparrow tumbled from its nest. He was moved with infinite compassion for the multitudes, reaching out to touch the troubled ones with His strong hands bringing health and healing to those in need.

What He did then He does now! He has not changed or altered in His capacity to remedy the wrongs of the world. Yet it is noteworthy that those He healed and restored to wholeness were always told to do one of three things. Some were to tell no one at all of what had taken place. Others were to go home quietly and tell only their immediate family of what great things God had done for them. The honor was to be given to the Lord. Their faith was not to be paraded as something special for the adulation of their associates. Still others were to report to the priest for confirmation of cleansing.

This is a matter of utmost importance! If and when our Father does bestow health and healing upon His people, its main purpose is to honor His greatness and to be used the better to serve His people.

The great peril is that instead it often leads to insidious pride and personal aggrandizement. Take the case of King Hezekiah, who was healed of his terminal illness: His tragic end was unmitigated sorrow and dreadful disaster for himself, his family, and his entire nation. The same can occur today. Read very solemnly 2 Kings chapter 20.

If, as we are told clearly, our bodies are in truth the temple (the residence) of God's Holy Spirit, then we are under obligation to Christ to care for them in a proper way. They are not ours to be abused or misused. This whole subject has been dealt with in some

of my previous books, especially in *Taming Tension*
and *Walking With God.*

When we turn our attention to wealth, precisely the
same basic principles apply. "Why do you want to be
rich?" "What end will your assets serve?" "What do
you intend to do with the monetary power put at your
disposal?"

It is common for some Christian leaders today to
use wealth as a means of trying to impress the secular
world with their own achievements. They seem to feel
that the "big splash," whatever form it takes, will
make the world sit up and take notice. The irony of it
all is that worldly society is so preoccupied with its
own pursuits that it could not care less what kind of
carnival show the Christians are staging with their
flashy lifestyle.

All of this stands in stark contrast to the character
and conduct of Christ. He who came from the incredible majesty of the eternal sovereignty of the universe
deliberately made Himself poor and served among us
so that we in turn might become the beneficiaries of
His generosity. He calls us, if we are to be His disciples, to do the same.

Any capacity that anyone may have to accumulate
wealth or amass money is a gift from God. We are not
"self-made" people. That is an absolute lie and delusion. As God's children it is expected of us to use our
assets, entrusted to our care, for the well-being and
benefit of others. Whatever we accumulate during our
brief few years is to be seen as a trust which we are
responsible to administer with wisdom and generosity toward God and man.

We are not here to impress others with our possessions. They are not just bestowed upon us for our
personal leisure and pleasure. Anyone who leads us to

believe this is a liar and charlatan. Our responsibility is to honor Christ with our income and to share generously with those He lays upon our path to help and to heal.

As Christ taught so very emphatically, those whom He finds faithful in their management of small amounts will soon be entrusted with ever-larger grants from His good hands. Try it and find out for yourself. Our faith is to extol Him—not us.

Faith comes to us as a magnificent gift from God. It is intended to be invested in His own impeccable character. In this way it brings Him enormous pleasure, for thus it demonstrates to the whole world how totally trustworthy He is. Faith was never intended to be used for man's own self-adulation, as so many leaders would have us believe.

4

Love
of Self

In living memory there has never been such a selfish generation as this one. It is sometimes called the "me" generation. Its main preoccupation is self-love in all of its most insidious manifestations. It explains in large measure why we have a society in such chaos and confusion.

The whole philosophy of self-love has swept through Western society like a raging inferno that consumes the finer qualities of human conduct. The noble aspects of life in which people truly care for others and work for their well-being have to a great extent been extinguished in the crude crucible of our crass culture.

In very large measure the responsibility for this tragic turn of events must be laid at the doorstep of the contemporary church. This may seem to be a shocking statement, but it is nevertheless true. The concept of human beings loving themselves is as ancient as creation itself. The compelling desire to put one's own interests first, above all others, has never diminished since the day Cain murdered Abel in a fit of rage and envy.

What must be remembered is that the clear call of God to us in Christ cuts diametrically across this ancient attitude of aggressive attrition. Jesus told us very plainly and in unmistakable terms to love those who are our enemies, to bless those who curse us, to do good to those who hate us, and to pray for those who persecute us.

But most of us just don't do this!

For the majority of mankind it is a case of "dog eat dog." The fierce law of the jungle prevails, in which people push for the top and care little who is crushed beneath their boots. The single most compelling consideration is simply *"What is in it for me?"*

It has been pointed out in the preceding chapters that some church leaders themselves seek for power, prestige, and prominence in the pulpit. Christian leaders of every sort subscribe to the success syndrome both in their own personal behavior and in the conduct of their followers. Others of them even encourage their audiences to use their faith for the ulterior purpose of promoting their own selfish ends.

So it is not difficult to understand how the appeal to love of self would fit comfortably into the contemporary world. The teachers and preachers, writers and lecturers, entertainers and musicians who promulgate this perverse and destructive philosophy find a ready reception for their views wherever they go.

They are popular with the public, riding the wave of modern thought that is said to represent the new age.

Anyone who dares to suggest today that the very character of God is the exact opposite to that of modern man is said to be out of touch with the times. When some of us cry out to our generation that the very Person of God, revealed to us in Christ, is one of *self-giving, selflessness, self-losing, self-sacrifice,* and *self-sharing*, we are laughed at in open derision, regarded with scorn, thought to be eccentrics.

After all, the contemporary catchwords both in society and in Christian circles are *self-respect, self-fulfillment, self-gratification, self-esteem,* and *self-affirmation*—in short, *self-love*. Nor do various leaders hesitate to press these aspirations upon their people.

From where do these teachings and theories come? In large part they have been spawned by men and women who despised God and disdained His Word. Among these are psychologists and sociologists of every stripe.

The people who have penetrated the Christian community with their false teaching and destructive ideas are often ensconced in our so-called halls of learning. They occupy positions of prominence in our colleges, universities, seminaries, and even some Bible institutes. Using very subtle, persuasive language with a thin veneer of Scriptural terminology, they appear to be so plausible while actually promulgating worldly philosophies which are diametrically opposite to the eternal truth revealed to us in Christ.

The whole concept of self-love has become so deeply entrenched in Christian teaching today that it has changed the entire complexion of Christian counseling. Television broadcasts, church seminars, scores of bestselling books, lucrative lectures, and endless radio programs all exploit the human desire and natural human inclination to love one's self. Little wonder that our leaders love to emphasize this concept in their appeal to the public—it is bound to be a sure seller!

The end result is that we now have a comfortable contemporary church that is very content to sit back and relax happily in the comfortable ease of its own padded pews. The stirring challenge of seeing God's people as an embattled body of believers standing strong on enemy territory, then marching on to victory while overcoming the opposition arrayed against Christ, is no longer here. Our leaders for the greater part have come to an easy accommodation with the world.

It is, to use a secular saying, a case where "If you can't lick them, join them!" This has become the hallmark of our times. Because certain secular concepts so quickly mesmerize the masses in the world, it is assumed that the same approach and same strategy can be used in the church.

In many areas of Christian activity and teaching the common people have been seduced by their leaders to believe that it is imperative to turn to psychology or psychiatry or other sociological programs for mental or emotional healing. Because those in the pulpit do not themselves know the life of the Risen Christ in their own experience, they lead their followers to try to find help in the ways of the world . . . the broad, barren paths that lead ultimately to self-delusion and self-destruction.

To understand how this happens it is essential that we understand clearly the consequences of love for self. Some of them are explained here. They may very well alert the reader to see precisely what peril he or she faces through this subtle subversion.

Self-love invariably leads to intense selfishness. If encouraged, it produces a personality in which the main preoccupation is self-interest. The character is corrupted by always turning inward to indulge one's own interests and to gratify one's own desires. This is done without due respect for other people no matter how damaging the conduct may be.

This is the attitude of life which says in so many words, "What is in it for me?" "If I feel like it, I'll do it; if I don't, I won't!" "Who cares?"

This outlook has no sense of responsibility whatever to others. It simply has no concern for the common good of the community. It has no intention of making any worthwhile contribution to society. The world is its oyster. It will pry open the shell to extract all it can.

This stands in sharp contrast to the call of Christ that we should in fact be those who do care very deeply for others. We do have an obligation as His people to lift up the fallen, to help the downtrodden, to bring rest to the weary, to restore the stricken of the earth.

Self-love, if indulged and pandered to, produces enormous personal pride. Almost always this is accompanied by arrogance in attitude and a certain crude haughtiness in behavior. Such individuals are often very difficult. There is an element of self-protection in such people which keeps others at arm's length. They are not easily approached and they are seldom open to any suggestions.

These attributes are, of course, the exact opposite of humility and meekness, which God our Father considers of such paramount importance. In fact He sets Himself against the proud person. Nor does He deign to reside with, or even draw near to, the haughty in heart. How can He, when their will is set against His good will?

Self-love invariably leads to cruel conduct which does enormous damage. For example, in the area of social relationships, which can be so very precious, the self-serving person will exploit others for his or her own personal gratification. That which passes under the world's guise of love is most commonly nothing more than raw and corrupt lust. It not only demeans the other individual but actually destroys the integrity of the offender.

Again Christ calls us to abstain from such activities. He has nothing but our own best interests in mind. Yet our leaders would have us believe that it is possible to eat your cake and have it too. What a lie!

Self-love always ends up in chronic discontent. One has put himself on a pedestal. He lives in constant concern that he may be pushed off, insulted, or humiliated. There is neither peace nor contentment.

Yet Christ calls us to come and learn of Him. It is He who can produce within us a contrite spirit and humble heart. It is He who offers us rest and respite from the torture of self-love.

The above are but a few of the despicable attitudes of self-love which make it the exact antithesis to the character of Christ. Are we surprised then to discover why such behavior is an affront to the holiness of a loving, caring, compassionate Savior? Can we not see, even if only dimly, why such a life is said by God to be deep in darkness and spiritual death, enslaved to sin and self? Can we not grasp why such conduct is a grief to God the Holy Spirit? He must of absolute necessity convict the individual of sin, of righteousness, and of ultimate judgment to come.

But—and "but" is an important word just here—
some of our spiritual leaders will not warn their people
of this peril. They will not call them to turn from their
wicked ways. They will not beseech them to repent of
their wrongs. They will not entreat them to confess
their corruption. They will not alert them to come
to Christ and cast themselves upon His marvelous
mercy. They will not point out that only in Him is
there forgiveness for their past, a purging away of
their guilt, an offer of a brand-new life of utter selflessness from above.

Why? Why are these things not done? The answer
is simple yet startling: Because they themselves have
not received new life in Christ. They know Him not!

How can they introduce anyone else to Christ if
they themselves have not yet met the Master? The
awesome truth is that literally hundreds upon hundreds of ministers, teachers, and leaders of all sorts in
the Christian community have never come to Christ.

"To come to Christ" means to put absolute and
implicit confidence in His character and in His own
personal commitments to us made in His name in His
Word. It is a personal, positive response to the utter
integrity of His Person.

"To believe on Christ" is to actually commit one's
whole self to Him in such a manner that He is given
complete access to every area of life. He is literally
taken into the life of the believer. He shares every
aspect of it. He becomes the integral and compelling
dynamic of daily living. This essentially is what is
meant by Christ in me and me in Christ. There is a
complete exchange and interchange of His character
with mine, so that in effect I become re-made, recreated, re-formed into His image.

This is the only possible way in which a selfish, self-centered, self-serving, self-loving individual can ever be changed into a self-less, self-giving son of God. It is the miracle of being born from above. It is a transformation more beautiful than any bloom that ever burst from a brown bud or any butterfly that ever crawled out of a drab cocoon.

Such a soul, overwhelmed with gratitude and love for the generosity of such a gracious, caring God, cannot help but love Christ. The compelling desire now, above all others, is to do His Will, obey His instructions, and live in joyous harmony with Him.

This is the supreme secret to knowing, loving, and enjoying Christ. Nothing else in all the world can even come near this magnificent relationship between God and man. Life in communion with Him becomes a magnificent adventure in which His utter reliability and gracious faithfulness are demonstrated every day.

On this basis our confidence in Christ expands. Our quiet faith in our Loving Father increases. Our sure sensitivity to His gracious Spirit is enhanced. Our lives become strong, sure, and serene.

In His strength we go out quietly to serve our generation. No longer lovers of self, we now love others and gladly lay down our lives for them as Christ lays down His life for us.

5

The Decadence of the Western World

It is generally assumed by Western nations, both in Europe and North America, that their culture and society are the most civilized in all of human history. This is simply not the case. Any people who conduct their social life in the way we do are extremely decadent.

High-rise towers of steel and glass that tower into the sky, jet aircraft that cross continents in hours, television reception that puts the whole earth at our fingertips in seconds—these may be a measure of high technology, but they mean nothing in measuring the morals of a people.

Especially is this the case when a people are so given to self-love and self-indulgence as to destroy the very fabric of their own world by greed, gross behavior, and personal gratification. A society which actually encourages all sorts of promiscuous relationships for sheer pleasure, then covers the consequences by world-wide abortions in the millions, is gross and bestial. Even dogs and donkeys will not do that.

A people whose population is so permissive that it allows easy access to destructive drugs in the form of alcohol, nicotine, hallucinatory drugs, and other chemical stimulants and sedatives is headed for sure destruction. Ruined minds, twisted personalities, irresponsible behavior, crime, and violence are all the end product of this scene. Increasingly, millions are caught up in the carnage.

A people whose chief end in life is leisure and pleasure will not long survive the onslaught of more disciplined cultures. How can we compete with others who take the trouble to work hard and produce superior products out of a social sense of personal achievement? Our generation seeks maximum wages for minimum work. In the workplace the idea is to beat the system and outfox the employer.

In government, education, and social relationships of all sorts, outright corruption, distortion of truth, and failure to carry out personal commitments are common conduct. It is considered clever, sharp, and sophisticated to "put one over" on other people. The individual is no longer respected for his or her integrity or decency but rather for the ability to "make a deal," even if the most subtle subterfuge is used.

Rapidly the Western world is rejecting absolute moral standards which once were considered the hallmark of a so-called Christian society. Instead young people are taught that anything goes; bend the law; take all you can get away with—just don't get caught.

The ultimate evil is not to do wrong but to be found out. Use others to your own end.

Our Christian leaders themselves emerge from this corrupt culture. It is the milieu which has shaped their mind-set and conditioned their thinking. Many have been so much a part of the process that they accept it as the norm. Having grown up in it, they are neither startled nor grieved by the world in which they minister. Unless by the remarkable transformation of God's presence in their own personal lives they look out on the social scene with His perspective, they are not alarmed by the chaos nor saddened by the confusion and carnage.

This explains why in so many places the pastors and teachers are well-nigh silent about social ills. They make no strong stand against those elements that are destroying their people. They carry no deep conviction about the corruption all about them. They will not risk a confrontation with the forces of evil. Their silence gives tacit approval to the wrong influences and human philosophies which are tearing us to pieces.

The leaders are fearful lest they be branded eccentrics, puritans, or prophets of doom. They much prefer to be popular.

When we turn momentarily to consider the life of Christ, we are startled by the stand which He took in His society. He was so distinct and so different from His contemporaries that He stated unashamedly, "I AM TRUTH." Yes, His whole life was one of utter integrity lived out amid a culture of complete corruption, a world system in which even a cynic like Pilate the Roman governor had to ask, "What is truth?" He had never encountered it until he confronted it face-to-face in Christ. Are we surprised that just a few hours earlier this same Jesus had stood on a hill overlooking Jerusalem and wept unashamedly over the wickedness and wretchedness of the great capital?

Christ called His followers not only to *truth* as it was found in Himself but also to a *way* and to a *life* that were distinctly different and divergent from the corrupt culture of His times. He told them plainly that it would be a constricted calling which few would find palatable or appealing. He stated emphatically that the great majority of men and women would prefer to follow the popular, broad, all-encompassing trends of the times that lead to sure destruction. It was the broad way, the easy way, the enticing way.

Christ made it astonishingly hard for most of His contemporaries to follow Him. The demands made upon those who decided to be His disciples were very lofty. He never promised them ease, luxury, or self-indulgence. His call was to a tough life of enormous self-sacrifice. He warned those who wished to walk with Him that there was a formidable price to pay for such a privilege. The cost would be counted in terms of tribulation, alienation, personal abuse and hatred by their antagonists.

All of this is a far cry indeed from that made by some Christian leaders in our Western world. Their false assertion is that most people really do want to come to Christ. It is as easy to join the church as to join a social club. What a lie! Yet not a lie!

The contemporary church imposes almost no rigid standards of behavior upon its adherents or members. Most of the leaders are afraid to do so lest they be labeled stern legalists. The current concept is that Christians should be so warm, so loving, so sweet, so tolerant that almost anything goes. The idea of calling a congregation to abstain from the corrupt practices of our culture becomes increasingly rare and hard to find even in the most conservative churches. There is almost no clear-cut distinction of any kind between the so-called Christian and his or her non-Christian associates. Virtually the only difference is that the former may show up at a church on a Sunday, whereas the latter lie between the sheets on the bed.

Pastors, ministers, evangelists, and teachers are so eager to be liked by their congregation, so keen to be popular with their parishioners, so determined to be accepted by their society that they refuse to cry out against its evils as did the prophets of old. They live in abject fear of being despised or rejected of men as was the Master. They will go instead to great lengths to insinuate themselves into society in order to be "one of the good old boys," hail, well-met, and having achieved a happy rapport with the world around them.

Laypeople have every right to take a very hard look at their spiritual leaders. They are entitled to ask some very tough questions of those who pretend to be their shepherds. They need to know for certain whether those occupying their pulpits are men and women of truth or falsehood.

Many, many Christians are extremely gullible. They will accept almost any teaching as long as it is offered to them in a smooth and plausible package. Altogether too few study God's Word enough to know the difference between truth and deception. Little wonder that they fall prey to imposters!

Though our contemporary Christian leaders use many methods to try to accommodate themselves and their people to our decadent society, the net impact is minimal. It was said of former times: "The church was never so powerful in the world as when she had nothing to do with the world." The reason for this is that it was clearly understood that the two were set in total contradistinction from each other. Christians knew unmistakably that they had a deep allegiance to Christ, whereas the world rejected Him and despised His verities. God's people, while "in the world," were not of it, for they knew they were on enemy ground. And the ultimate assignment given to them from The Most High was to penetrate that realm, as light does darkness, or salt does decay, in order to claim territory for God at great personal cost.

This is a far cry from the current world view of many church leaders. The present approach is one of coming to terms with the times, of trimming our attitudes to conform to modern trends in society, of using worldly means and worldly methods to try to right the wrongs that are destroying us. The catchword of our generation is *comfortable.* Leaders pour out puerile pap from their pulpits lest they make their listeners uncomfortable. They will not dare to make a bold, brave stand for Christ lest they come under attack from the media or the community. Even if truth is trampled underfoot, and righteousness is repudiated, they still remain silent. They dare not be distinct or different.

In large part the reason for this is the current seduction of both the church and society by the teachings of psychology and psychiatry. Sociologists are having a field day in human affairs. They have deluded the masses to believe that men and women are really not responsible for their wrongdoing. They insist instead that wrongdoers are victims of poor parenting, adverse environmental influences, or genetic inheritance.

People are said to be "sick" but are never declared
to be sinners. Such words as "sin," "sinful," and "sinner"
are almost becoming archaic in our language except
among a very small circle of hard-core Christians who
still accept God's special disclosure about the human
condition. These people are regarded by society as
fanatics who are out on the fringe of things. They have
no part in the mainstream of modern thought.

This whole concept of people being "sick" has so
permeated the rationale of our decadent society that
it even conditions all of our judicial system. Men and
women can commit the most violent crimes and indulge
in the most heinous atrocities against society and still
be exonerated. On the basis of psychological philosophy the offender is declared to be innocent and not
responsible for his or her despicable behavior. Both
jury and judges conclude that a minimal penalty should
be imposed. So the criminal laughs at the law and
despises any ideas of decency.

Then in dismay the public cries out, "What is
wrong?" "Where is justice?" "Why can't we have law
and order?"

The answer is that our Christian leaders have be-
trayed us. The predators in our pulpits have promul-
gated such pernicious principles based on human philosophy that righteousness, justice, and truth are no
longer a watchword to our people.

As the Word of God declares vehemently, they call
good evil and they call evil good. The laity in their
ignorance and confusion are led to believe a lie. They
assume they are being taught truth when in fact it is
a travesty of the truth.

The highly esteemed halls of learning in universities, colleges, and seminaries turn out leaders who
love to make people comfortable in their corruption.

Their chief objective is to have people believe that everything is beautiful in our culture when in fact it is becoming bestial.

On every hand we have people calling out for us to condone the corruption in our world. We are told to be tolerant of others in a multicultural society even if their beliefs and behaviors bring us down into destruction. We are urged to wink at wrong and sweep subversion under the carpet of contemporary broadmindedness, while all the time we teeter on the cliff's edge of anarchy. All sorts of strange voices cry out to insist on their entrenched civil liberties. They shout that they have every right to do wrong even if it demolishes human dignity, destroys the last remnant of social decency, and deprives others of their rights.

Amid all this mayhem it is surprising to see so many in positions of so-called Christian leadership actually align themselves with the forces of evil. There are many in various pulpits who actually subscribe to violence, revolution, and anarchy to attain social change. In the name of Christianity they promote anarchy and openly support subversive activity. By so doing, some of them are able to gather up a formidable following, who in turn deny others their right to do what is proper and good.

The ultimate conclusion that must be reached amid this confusion is to see distinctly that many of these leaders really do not know Christ. They have no personal acquaintance with Him. They do not live under His unction. They are not subject to His will. They do not subscribe to the lofty standards of human conduct He has set before us.

Because of this they do not see the great evils of our day in the white, intense light of His justice and righteousness. They cannot comprehend that it is man's

corruption and sin that took Him to the cross to pay
the ultimate penalty for our wrongdoing. They do not
understand His generous redemptive love which alone
can cleanse our past and preserve our present.

So they do not cry out against sin as sin. For they do
not see it as a crime against Christ, an evil against
others, or a betrayal of ourselves. Being blind themselves, they are leaders of the laity, who are also blind.

6

Peace, Peace— At Any Price

There is abroad in the world a tremendous ground swell of public sentiment that insists on peace. No other single word in the human language today carries with it the apparent power and persuasiveness so inherent in the term PEACE. The general public, both young and old and of almost every strata of society, speak glibly of peace. The entire human race yearns for it—indeed clamors for peace. Their multitudes hold peace conferences, peace marches, peace seminars, peace parades, and peace protests of a hundred sorts.

It is incredible that in a world so divided and at odds over most issues there should be such a unanimity of desire for peace. This longing for peace is much more than purely a political panacea for settling differences between nations. It reaches beyond the established national boundaries that govern diverse countries. It is a formidable force which takes on broad philosophical overtones, which insists that all people should blindly tolerate communal thinking on a worldwide basis.

All of this is understandable when viewed against the background of carnage and destruction of so many wars in human history. It is not surprising that human beings do seek peace when they pause to consider the awful waste and destruction that combat brings. They revolt at the suffering and sorrow involved in war. They recoil from the terror of an atomic exchange or the utter devastation of a nuclear or chemical holocaust. So "peace, peace at any price" becomes the common cry that ascends from the masses in increasing crescendo.

It is becoming the pivot point around which worldwide public opinion rotates with ever-accelerating momentum. There can be no doubt that the cry for peace will eventually demand the appearance of a prince of peace.

Sooner or later there will emerge in human history an individual of international acclaim who commands universal attention for his supposed devotion to the cause of peace. We already have the forerunners to such a leader in the selection of men or women who are awarded the Nobel Peace Prize. One sometimes wonders who it was who chose certain people for this honor, since their subsequent behavior has often been less than peaceable. And in some cases their prestige has been used to promote controversy in the human community, not accord.

Nevertheless these individuals serve as indicators to all of us that worldwide peace is a delusion. There can be no such thing as universal accord. Anyone asserting that this is possible is promulgating a lie. As God's special revelation makes so clear, men shall cry, "Peace! Peace! when there is no peace" (Jeremiah 6:14; 8:11).

It is essential that we should understand why this is so. At the very root of all human behavior lies the inescapable, inevitable determination of unshakable self-interest. This powerful force conditions human conduct. It finds common expression in self-advancement, self-love, and self-satisfaction. In a word, it is basic selfishness serving one's own selfish ends.

This principle is what sets brother against brother, children against parents, neighbor against neighbor, community against community, nation against nation, ideology against ideology. It is therefore absurd to assume, much less suggest, that all men can live together in peace. It simply cannot be done.

Yet the astonishing fact is that an increasing number of leaders in religious circles are claiming that worldwide peace is possible. Leaders in almost every area of Christendom are calling to their people to support their peace initiatives. Peace is offered as the great panacea that will resolve all the tumult of our times.

It is astonishing that when Christ came to earth, His advent was heralded with the ringing proclamation "Peace on earth, good will to men." He, God's own Son, the Prince of Peace, the God of all Peace, had actually appeared among men. Yet He was neither received nor recognized as such. Instead the human race chose to reject and despise Him. They turned to attack Him. Though He came bringing only gracious goodwill, they would have none of it. They considered Him their implacable enemy who must be destroyed at any cost. This they did with terrible cruelty and despicable cunning.

Are we surprised then when He stated categorically, "I came not to bring peace, but a sword"? Later He pointed out that anyone who followed Him and chose to live by His code of conduct would also suffer persecution, be hated vehemently, endure awful alienation, and undergo terrible tribulation. All of this came true not only for His disciples but also for the entire early church.

Why? Why have God's special people who name His name always come under attack? Why does the world in general disdain and despise Christians? Why should those who follow Christ and desire to live in peace so often find themselves under siege and at odds with their contemporaries?

In a word, it is because they are different! They do not conform to the common culture. They live by a set of standards which puts a priority upon serving God and others rather than their own self-interests. They tend to bring a sense of self-reproach upon those who prefer to live selfish lives. In any case evil always despises goodness; brutality always disdains beauty; falsehood always abhors truth.

So it is impossible to come to terms between the two. THERE CAN BE NO PEACE!

In light of the foregoing it is imperative to ask ourselves some hard questions about the predators in our pulpits who insist that we must have peace at any price. What is that price? What kind of peace do they have in mind? What will be the ultimate end of such a process? Do they really have our best interests in mind?

Unfortunately, and all too often, people with evil and ulterior motives, generally of a purely political nature, use the religious arena as a platform for their propaganda. It is not at all uncommon for Christian leaders to become caught up in social concerns to the point that they use their pulpits and popular appeal as a political instrument to influence public opinion.

Such men and women need to have their motives carefully examined. Are they engaging in this sort of activity for the true benefit of their followers or for personal acclaim? Do they see this as a means to warn others of impending danger in society or as a stepping stone for their own personal advancement? Are they genuinely interested in preserving their people from a political peril or is it another way to manipulate the masses and appeal to the mob instinct?

It is not uncommon for leaders who in the beginning of their careers were certainly called of God to serve His church have later been seduced to serve the state in a political dimension. They do not seem to see this as a step backward, but it is. It is not that they cannot serve society in the secular field, for they can, but that this is not their most high calling. Nor is it denied that great good can at times be done by Christians in public office or in some other secular field. But the fact remains that the demands of the public, or one's obligation to the employer, limit the full devotion of one's strength, energy, and talents to the service of God.

Besides all this, the allurement of larger monetary rewards holds a strange fascination that tempers the message of truth.

From the most ancient times the men and women who truly wished to be loyal to God have come into conflict with the culture of their era. It did not matter whether the confrontation was over wealth, social mores, false religions, paganism, political philosophies, or simple faith in the Living God. Amid all of these tensions they were called to be a separate people with a totally different perspective on life and its meaning from that of their contemporaries.

Where the peril lay for these people, as it does for us, is in the leadership among God's people. Do we have powerful men and women of faith in Christ who will not compromise with the corruption of their decadent society? Do we have individuals with noble standards like Joseph, Samuel, Daniel, and Paul who simply will not submit to the seduction of their society nor crumple under the persecution of their opponents? Do our under-shepherds stand for truth that can preserve their people from the perils of false peace initiatives that come in many guises?

After all, so-called "peace" is an all-embracing term which now covers unification, accommodation, or even regimentation of diverse elements in the social scene. For example, we speak very freely of military peace, of political accord, of religious ecumenism, of social solidarity, of industrial settlements between management and labor, and of spiritual unity amid all its diversity.

In each arena there are advocates who work tirelessly to bring about the imposition of certain views upon their contemporaries. It is here that Christians are bound to become involved in the social process. It is not possible to stand apart, detached from whatever changes are at work in the world. A stand must be made. So it is that we are fully entitled to ask as laity, Where do our leaders stand? Where are their loyalties?

It is common knowledge that all through the long
and tortured history of the church its people have
paid an enormous price for their love and loyalty to
Christ. From generation to generation God's people
have endured great suffering for His sake. Nor is
this any less true today than it was in former times.
The persecution of Christians goes on with unabated
vehemence in various countries throughout the world.
In large measure this is because these brave spirits
will not settle for peace at any price. They refuse to
come to terms with social systems—whether political, religious, cultural, or academic—that demand
they should deny the Living Christ.

Yet it must be stated that almost always there have
been insidious leaders within the Christian community who were traitors to the truth in Christ. These
so-called "shepherds" were and still are those who for
either personal or political or social advantage mislead their followers into servitude or seduction to
strange beliefs and false ideologies.

The vehicle used to accomplish this is the ever-
plausible "peace process." As pointed out at the beginning of this chapter, peace has an enormous appeal to
common people. So in the name of peace and under
the guise of goodwill tempered by tolerance, Christians are everywhere urged and encouraged to accept
all sorts of destructive ideas and false influences that
may be their undoing.

These take a hundred forms, far too numerous to
list here in detail. But most of them come under one or
more of the following categories: universalism in religion; the belief that all spiritual concepts lead to God;
the omniscience of the occult and mysticism; plausible political philosophies that provide for the welfare of all; academic and scientific humanism that

exalts man's intellect; gross materialism; scientific evolutionary hypotheses; the subtle appeal of hedonism as man's chief end in life.

Each of these in its own peculiar way can exert a strong attraction for various people. Nor are our leaders exempt from their falsehood. If they are caught up in the excitement or deception of any of these influences, they in turn will use their pulpits or platforms to try to propagate their message. Herein lies the greatest peril for God's people. So often it is assumed by the laity that simply because an individual in the Christian community occupies a position of prominence, what he or she has to say is authentic.

Not so! A hundred times no!

We have preachers, evangelists, teachers, educators, radio broadcasters, publishers, authors, television personalities, and a score of other spokesmen who claim to speak for Christ while actually destroying His people with diabolical deception. Their sweet, peaceable pronouncements sound so plausible while all the time they tear the truth out of men's lives.

It may well be asked, What is the antidote for this devastation? Where do we find the faith and fortitude to perceive falsehood and confront the counterfeits? How do we know when we are being deluded?

The answer is astonishingly simple: Get into God's Word daily.

Search its truth in diligent study. Give yourself completely to the control of Christ. Come to know Him intimately. Discover for yourself the wonder of His impeccable character. Learn firsthand of our Father's enormous love and care for you. Invest your wholehearted faith in Him. Determine to do His will and comply with His clear commands. Find out for yourself how wonderful it is to walk with Him in love and loyalty. See how serene and strong you can be in Him.

This sort of person is not easily misled by false imposters who come crying "Peace! Peace!" when there is no peace. For they have found their peace in Christ. Read carefully John 14.

This personal inner peace is completely different from the popular peace which the world speaks about. It has been discussed in great detail in my book *A Gardener Looks at the Fruits of the Spirit*, so it will not be dealt with here again. But this superb inner peace that comes to the Christian from the abiding presence of the Risen Christ is that which can sustain him amid every adversity in life. It is that which can provide serenity in the most violent storms of his earthly sojourn.

7

Emotional Experience Versus Disciplined Obedience

Second only to the success syndrome, the Western world's greatest preoccupation is sensationalism. The devotion of the masses to whatever is spectacular, exciting, and highly stimulating to the senses defies description. Crowds in their uncounted millions mass in hordes like ants or flies hovering over a dead carcass to participate in a program which arouses their emotions or stimulates their excitement.

The astonishing thing is that not only will they go to great lengths to reach the scene of activity, but they also gladly pay a high price to be a participant spectator. This is true of sporting events of every kind, musical presentations, theatrical performances, political rallies, or even so-called "religious revivals."

The Western world is essentially a spectator society in which emotional experience is considered a must for the masses.

The use of huge stadiums to accommodate the crowds, the worldwide radio and television networks employed to reach uncounted millions of listeners or viewers, the universal distribution of literature, advertising, and promotion to capture the public's attention—all these sweep up multitudes in a sort of mass following and at times mass hysteria. Almost overnight, heroes and heroines are made or demolished by the media.

It matters not whether the star be a football player, a racing driver, an actor, a politician, or a preacher—one day he may be a public idol and the next day a villain. We are a people who will offer up any human sacrifice to our insatiable lust for entertainment and selfish desire for emotional experience. Show business is big business; it involves big money. Almost anything is accepted as long as it produces a stimulating high for the spectator.

This concept of excitement and highly charged emotional experience has made an enormous impact on the twentieth-century church. It is so much a part of our culture that the situation simply cannot be otherwise. First of all the tremendous attraction of sports, theater, politics, or other show business draws the masses away from less sensational spiritual activities. Most moderns consider the church pretty dull and drab. Compared to the high-powered sensationalism of the sports arena or stage or silver screen, the average Christian congregation is considered dead, dead, dead.

Secondly, many Christian leaders have come to the conclusion that the only possible way to compete with the contemporary world attractions is to adopt their style and methods. So it is not the least surprising to see huge and ornate structures of steel, glass, and concrete erected to attract and accommodate crowds. It is not a bit shocking to see Christian leaders put on dazzling programs with glamorous people to equal anything in Hollywood or New York. It is not astonishing to hear rock music and syncopated sounds in our sanctuaries. The average churchgoer fully expects the person in the pulpit to be very polished, a high-profile performer who can entertain hilariously with humor, wit, and sometimes silly stories.

In many of the smaller churches where there is less opportunity for people to put on a pompous show, leaders turn to more intimate types of exciting entertainment. They have highly charged group encounters where body contact stimulates the senses. They indulge in "open dialogue" in which participants let it all hang out in emotional empathy. Soft, sensual music or introverted passive periods of meditation are used to try to stimulate exciting sensations. Even the dance is used to arouse the senses.

The list goes on and on. The main objective is simply to satisfy the crowds. Their demand for an exciting experience, no matter whether public or private, must be met. The end result is that millions of earnest, seeking souls have been given a bowl full of sensationalism but scarcely a crumb of truth. They come with searching spirits that can only be truly satisfied by the presence of the Living Christ. They go away deceived into believing that they have been touched by God's Spirit when in fact it was largely a sham and show.

Proof that this is so lies in the conduct of their lives and the quality of their characters. Thousands upon thousands of these dear deluded souls live like yo-yos. Today they are high on an ecstatic upbeat of excitement. Tomorrow they are down in the depths of dullness and despair. Nothing very exciting is happening, so they feel flat and forsaken of God. The sum total of their spiritual experience is a series of signs, wonders, and spurious manifestations of one sort or another. In large measure their leaders are responsible for this terrible travesty.

An even more serious dimension of their spiritual deception lies in the fact that they are often led to believe a lie. Exciting revelations, stimulating prophecies, erotic encounters (often counterfeited by false teaching), and spurious spirits lead the gullible ones to do the most despicable deeds. Yet they insist that they have done so under the guidance of "the Spirit." One must ask, "What spirit?" and "Whence does he come?"

The above behavior and belief is much more common in the contemporary church than many people realize. It is a delusion and deception. Emotional experience is no substitute for the knowledge of the true and living Lord Jesus Christ. He can be known only by obedience to His Word. That is the ultimate test of truth.

Christ Himself addressed this whole matter in one of the most important and serious statements made in all of Scripture:

> Not every one that saith unto me, Lord, Lord, shall enter into the kingdom of heaven, but he that doeth the will of my Father which is in heaven.
>
> Many will say to me in that day, Lord, Lord, have we not prophesied in thy name? and in thy

name have cast out devils? and in thy name done many wonderful works? And then will I profess unto them, I never knew you; depart from me, ye that work iniquity (Matthew 7:21-23).

It is not the sensational speakers, or the startling leaders who perform wonders, or the exciting individuals who ostensibly exorcise evil spirits, manufacture miracles, and astound their audiences with signs and wonders who necessarily know Christ. Rather, it is the persons who in implicit obedience comply with His commands and consistently do His will. The two are poles apart. Yet often the crowds much prefer the theatrics and carnival atmosphere created by the charismatic leader.

The argument is often advanced that a skeptical, cynical society will not come to Christ unless they see spectacular signs and wonders to prove His power. But in His own day He told the nonbelievers that they simply would not believe Him despite all the authority of His words or the demonstrations of His power. So again the suggestions and statements of our leaders need to be carefully examined. Are they truly servants of God or merely entertainers who can capture the adulation of an audience?

A most compelling consideration is to inquire, "Where are all these thousands of converts whom these leaders claim to bring to Christ? Where are the crowds who are supposed to be healed or cured? Why are there not multitudes making an enormous impact on their communities?" Careful research has shown that only about 2 percent of these dear deluded people have been brought into a vital contact with the Living Christ, and into an enduring life of love.

In view of all this, the layperson who truly longs to know God, who wishes to walk with Christ in humility, must look elsewhere. The show-biz brand of Christianity will never assuage his deep longing to know God in reality.

The sum total of a person's spiritual pilgrimage must be more, much more, than a succession of ecstatic emotional experiences. The Master calls His followers into a life of quiet faith and calm fortitude in company with Himself. He asks us to enter into His sufferings in helping to bear the burdens of His earth children. He desires that above all else, at great personal cost, we should be willing to discipline ourselves to do His will and joyously comply with His wishes. In this practical way we daily demonstrate our love for Him and our concern for others around us whom we serve.

The Christian's life in Christ is not a staged performance put on to impress other people. Nor is it a dramatic demonstration of our special talents to entertain or astonish our contemporaries. Nor is it an exhibition of exciting experiences intended to arouse the admiration of our associates.

The Christian's life is a dynamic demonstration of the divine and supernatural life of Christ Himself in the conduct and character of a common man or woman. It is the supernatural rebirth and recreation of a soul deep in darkness brought into the life and light and love of God our Father. It is the wonder and beauty of a spirit once enslaved to sin but now set free to follow Christ in lifelong loyalty. It is the person who in strength and serenity is led daily by God's gracious Spirit in the paths of righteousness.

This is the layperson whom God can use in wondrous ways to accomplish His purposes on the planet. Such individuals are totally available to Christ to carry out

His work in the world. These are the people who are in truth light amid the darkness of our decadence, salt amid the corruption of our culture, and bearers of peace and stability amid the turmoil and tension of our times.

The responsibility of the leaders in our pulpits is to see that such people do occupy his or her pews. It is their duty to focus their followers' attention upon Christ and not upon themselves or their activities. Their chief end in life should be to lead others to love God with all their will, strength, and spirit.

Sad to say, this is often not done. Many who are in positions of influence prefer to have their followers become devotees of themselves. They love to bask in the affection and adulation which others lavish upon them for one reason or another.

One of the most insidious and widespread means used to this end is the current craze of pastoral counseling which has swept through the church. Again, it is a page lifted from the casebook of the psychologist or psychiatrist. The intimate personal encounter, the increasing dependence on human interaction, the sympathetic ear and inevitable emotional involvement—all these cater to the self-interests of both parishioner and pastor.

What most pastors and counselors appear to forget is that they are in fact supplanting the work of God the Holy Spirit. They are usurping the place of God's Counselor in convicting men and women of sin and righteousness and judgment to come. They are trying to play the role of little gods to those who are under their care.

God does not get His glory or His honor from this human interaction. Little wonder that so many leaders are exhausted and burned out by the endless deluge of defilement poured out upon them by counselees! Day and night they listen to a litany of despair that darkens their own souls and discourages their own spirits. Instead they should lift up Christ before the whole congregation and proclaim His Word with power for all to hear and obey.

When this is done with faithfulness and integrity, God the Holy Spirit will take the Word and use it to enlighten, edify, and convict the whole congregation. He will be the divine Counselor who remedies the wrongs among God's people. It is He who can bring to a whole community the profound sense of sin and need for God's mercy. It is He who in His sovereign grace can reshape the whole fabric of society. This is the true essence of a spiritual awakening. It is the quickening of human spirits with life from above, a beautiful enterprise which many long to see.

From time to time during the present century Christians have been privileged to see God do His own wondrous work in the world. The great revivals that took place in such widely scattered areas as Wales, East Africa, and Indonesia were not staged or contrived by man. They were the sovereign acts of The Most High God. They were a dramatic demonstration of God's divine presence made evident upon the earth without human manipulation.

If these are to come again in the Western world, the steps needed are clearly stated in God's Word. And those who should take them first, as an example to the laity, are the leaders in our Christian community. These are the ones who should show us how to humble ourselves before Christ, how to pray for His presence to move among us, how to seek His face until He is pleased to smile upon us in blessing and beneficence,

how to turn from our wicked ways in true contrition of
spirit to follow Him in loving loyalty.

This is the true role of our leaders.

Only when they discharge this duty with courage
will God be pleased to hear from heaven. Then He will
forgive our wrong and wicked ways. Then He will heal
our land and restore our society to one of decency and
dignity under His direction.

Part II

THE ROLE OF THE LAITY:
THE COST OF FOLLOWING CHRIST

And He (Jesus) said to them all, "If any man will come after me, let him deny himself, and take up his cross daily, and follow me."
        —Luke 9:23

Christianity has not been tried and found wanting. Christianity has been found difficult, and left untried!

        —G.K. Chesterton

1

The
Sacrifice
of Self-Will

If any person is going to follow Christ in wholehearted allegiance, he must clearly understand His
character. It simply is not enough for us to be told
about His actions in a historical narrative. Jesus the
Christ is not just a person who came on the scene as
another prophet and spent a few brief years among
men being abused, as most prophets are.

He is the very Person of God, who is from everlasting to everlasting, without beginning and without
termination. He is God, very God, all-knowing, all-
wise, all-powerful, who of His own will set His celes-
tial splendors aside and took on Himself for a few brief
years our human form. His was a perfect life, lived out
in an impeccable character, with a sinless personality.

This life He laid down deliberately in an act of enormous generosity to provide the perfect sacrifice of self-giving to propitiate for the awesome evil of all men everywhere. In demonstration of His own perfection and divine power He rose in utter triumph from the tomb. Death could not deter Him. Decomposition could not defile Him. Despair could not diminish His dynamic, eternal life. In utter majesty He ascended again to His position of power and prominence in the infinite realm of the unseen-yet-everlasting spiritual world. He is ever alive!

This Jesus—the Christ—is in total truth King of all Kings, Lord of all Lords, His Most High Majesty. His position of supreme sovereignty in the universe is seldom discerned and little understood by mortal men, most of whom live either in ignorance of Him or in open antagonism to His will and wishes. They are not aware that it is His dynamic, divine life which brings to all creatures everywhere all that is vital, wholesome, beneficial, and beautiful. Without His energy at work in the universe all would be darkness, death, and despair.

Jesus Christ came among us but briefly, yet in those few short years He revealed to us the essential character of God. He was the living embodiment of all those qualities which make life lovely, noble, joyous, and worthwhile. Amid the mayhem of man's despair, delusion, and darkness, He it is who always comes with hope, utter integrity, truth, and bright light.

For want of a better word in our human language the Spirit of God has chosen to call Him *love*. Yet He is not love in the mere sense of something sentimental, sweet, and rather romantic (though devotion to Him can arouse such sensations in the human soul) but much more. Yes, much more—more than can be found

88

anywhere in the human family . . . enduring compassion and utter comprehension.

This One, this Christ, this God who is said to be *love*, is in truth the eternal Friend, the enduring Benefactor, the suffering Saviour who ever shares Himself with us. His whole being—His entire Person, His sublime character—is one of caring and giving and bestowing on us benefits we do not deserve. It is His very nature to pour Himself out in endless blessing to all of His creation.

In Christ it is possible for us to both see and understand the wonder and the winsomeness of God's character. Its unique quality, which is so totally foreign to us earthlings, is its utter selflessness. In Christ we see the essence of a self-giving spirit. We can discern, even if only faintly, what it means to be self-sharing, self-sacrificing, and self-losing for the good of others in a continuous outpouring of life that is laid down for the well-being of others.

This gracious, magnanimous self-giving is the distinctive dynamic of Christ's love. It is the essential energy of His being. It is the powerful influence of His Person which counteracts all the evil, sin, and selfishness of human society.

It follows, then, that when He calls us into His company it is expected of us that we too shall become people of that caliber. His supreme desire is that those who are to be His people should display the same qualities of character which He does. If we are to call ourselves Christians ("like Christ"), then it is incumbent upon us to be like Christ not only in our outward conduct but also in our inmost character.

Christ spoke much about "the glory of God." He longed to share it with His associates. He prayed the Father to bestow it upon His followers as He Himself had revealed it to them. This "glory of God" is nothing else but the very character of Christ. His impeccable character is His supreme glory. It is His unique caliber of life and conduct which set Him apart from and far above His creation.

So when the Master invited men and women to come to Him and to follow Him, He was in truth calling them to an entirely new sort of life. The old ways would no longer do. The old attitudes would have to change. The old selfish, self-centered character would have to be completely altered.

In the very plain, simple, blunt language of His day He stated categorically, "If any man will come after me, let him deny himself and take up his cross daily and follow me" (Luke 9:23).

This implies clearly that to be in His company and walk in harmony with Him, having the same aims and objectives as He does, must entail self-denial. It sounds so simple to say, but it is the most difficult thing in all the world to do. It is a formidable cost to consider!

If we are to be allied with Christ, then obviously we cannot be in antagonism to Him. There can be no accord between His sublime selflessness and our petty, personal self-centeredness. Our selfishness must go. Our self-preoccupation has to be put to death. Our self-will has to be sacrificed to His great, generous goodwill!

This inherent human selfishness, which He commands us to abandon, finds expression in scores of different ways. Here are but a few: self-assertion, self-adulation, self-interest, self-pity, self-indulgence, self-gratification, self-avengement. These smooth, high-sounding terms so much esteemed by our human society are translated into rather startling language by God's Spirit in the Scriptures. There they are called "the works of the flesh"—namely adultery, fornication, lewdness, idolatry, hatred, dissension, wrath, anger, strife, seditions, envy, jealousy, etc.

It is common for human beings to object strongly to such a demand. They insist that they are just "doing what comes naturally" when they live this way. That is true—it is just the corrupt old human character. They insist they were simply born that way. That is true too! Man is born in sin and his whole personality is shaped in iniquity. They claim they can't help themselves. Nor can they! That is why they must come to Christ. They must cast themselves upon His compassion. They must trust Him to turn them around. And He will if they will it so.

Here is where the crunch comes.

Do we truly want to be different? Do we long to be remade in His likeness? Do we earnestly wish to be changed from our old character, so defiled, to His, so pure?

These are searching questions for the soul of man. They penetrate to the very center of his being. They call for radical and drastic changes in a person. They demand a complete re-creation of character.

The price to pay is daily self-denial.

The cost is to relinquish self-will to Christ's will.

The process is a painful crucifixion of one's self-centeredness in order to be free from self to follow Christ in love and joyous abandon.

In the more traditional language of the church this is called "conversion" or a complete turnaround of the entire life. It is not just a change of mind or an arousal of emotions toward God but a deep and dynamic redirection of the person's will.

In God's Word the term used for the will is "the heart." It is out of the unshakable decisions of the will (the heart of man) that come all the evils that are set in antagonism to Christ. So the will (self-will) must be touched and transformed by Christ coming into the individual's life if there is to be peace and harmony with Him.

Only in this way is it possible for Him to work in us both to will and to do of His good pleasure. So it can be seen that for this to happen there must be a complete capitulation of self-will to the control of Christ. It means coming under the direct government of God our Father. It involves our constant subservience to God's gracious Spirit in wholehearted (whole-willed) obedience daily.

Christ's call for us to renounce our self-interests in order to follow Him at first appears an impossible price to pay for this honor. This is because it entails total surrender. But the deep decision to do this can be accelerated when we begin to see clearly that we are slaves to ourselves. We are literally in bondage to our own crude, selfish, arrogant self-approbation. And this is really the source of most of our sorrow, stress, and pain in life. Oh, to be set free from the sinister shackles of our own self-interests! We are actually held captive by our own ego, pride, and self-esteem.

Christ comes to us and offers to set us free from our self-imprisonment. He sets the captive free to follow Him in glad self-renunciation. He breaks the bonds that bind us to ourselves and lets us take the high road of holiness with Him.

The reverse side of the challenge put to us is to discover the joy, beauty, and abundant delight to be found in doing Christ's commands. By degrees it dawns upon our dull spiritual awareness that none of His demands are to demean us or drive us into despair. Quite the opposite! Each is designed for our good. They are to enrich our lives, enlarge our experience, broaden our horizons, and enhance our well-being. They are actually for our maximum living. Consequently it becomes an honor and high calling to comply with His wishes. He becomes our very inspiration!

When this realization sweeps over our spirits it carries away our spiritual blindness as to what Christ's noble intentions are toward us. What from our old perspective appeared to be an enormous price of self-sacrifice can now be understood as a most special honor bestowed upon us by God, inviting us to come into His exclusive company. We see clearly that Christ is challenging us to a lofty life like His own, in which He calls us His companions, His friends, and yes, even more—His brothers and sisters.

For His part, He is fully prepared to enter any life opened to Him. He is ready to share Himself fully with any soul (person) who will receive Him as The Most High Majesty. He is delighted to take up residence within any human being who will in humility open up the innermost sanctum of his or her will and disposition to His presence.

On our part He asks that deliberately and very consistently we submit ourselves to His control. As this is done daily, it is He who empowers us to carry out His commands and to comply with His wishes. Our wholehearted compliance with His will is made possible because of our implicit confidence in His superb character. He will not delude or defraud us. He is totally trustworthy, so all is well.

This simple faith in His impeccable faithfulness to us opens up a whole wide world of joyous adventure with Him. We discover that as we deliberately make ourselves totally available to His noble purposes upon the planet, we are caught up with Him in joyous service and projects beyond our fondest hopes. He takes our little lives and uses them to His own great ends.

The sacrifice of self no longer looms large and costly in our calculations. Now we see it as our very reasonable response to the overtures of His love and concern for us. We begin to love as He loves, because He first loved us. We begin to grasp the eternal truth that the chief end of man is not to serve himself but to please Christ and to benefit others. We begin to see here the secret to serenity, the key to contentment, the dynamic for abundant living.

Day by day as by a deliberate act of our wills we choose to conform to Christ's wishes, to align ourselves with His aspirations, to cultivate His companionship, and to relish His presence within, we stumble over another great secret: He is simultaneously at work within us by His Spirit, conforming us to His own exquisite character. An exciting exchange is going on within our spirits, our souls, our very bodies. We are being recreated, remade into selfless, gracious, generous, great-hearted people. We are different, distinct, and separate from the self-oriented society around us.

The distinction does not lie in our adherence to some special creed or set of legal obligations. The difference lies in the dynamic of Christ's life within us and around us. He it is who now determines our deportment. We are no longer our own; we are His. Our conduct, our conversation, our characters are a living witness that He has complete command of our lives. What an honor! WHAT A HIGH AND NOBLE CALLING!

2

The Sacrifice of Our Priorities

The person who sincerely sets his will to be the Master's man or woman very quickly comes to see that Christ calls for a profound change in life's priorities. To put it in the plainest language, He not only demands a change of conduct, of character, and of conversation, but also of career. At least the place of prominence given to our careers in our everyday decisions has to be altered.

In the contemporary church with its worldly view of self-affirmation and self-fulfillment the challenge to sacrifice our careers for Christ is seldom mentioned. The more popular approach made to the masses by their leaders is that Christianity is a social activity that is sort of added on to one's secular career. It is hoped, of course, that this can be done with a minimum of disturbance to the daily activities demanded by one's normal lifestyle. It is seldom stated that to follow Christ calls for a radical upheaval in one's priorities, whatever they may be. This entails drastic dislocation of our devotion to those interests which formerly held first place in our day-to-day considerations.

This is a catastrophic challenge which very few people are prepared to accept. The cost seems too prohibitive, the sacrifice too severe. After all, it is argued that an individual may have spent the best years of his youth and huge sums of money in preparation for his life profession. Or he may have invested enormous amounts of time, energy, and concentration in qualifying for a certain career of his own choosing. Or through long years of apprenticeship, hard work, and excruciating experiences he may have reached a certain level of excellence in his field of endeavor. Surely he is not going to be asked to set all of this aside in order to do Christ's bidding!

If we turn our attention to the few brief years of our Lord's public life among His contemporaries, we are startled to see that this is what He demanded. He spoke to men like Matthew and Zaccheus. They were tough, hard-driving tax collectors who had amassed wealth through the corruption so common in their culture. There had to be a change. They had to leave the old life behind.

Jesus the Christ came into the lives of women like Mary Magdalene, who had plied her profession as a prostitute, and Martha, the house-proud homemaker. For both of these ladies at the extreme opposite ends of the social spectrum the Master called for a dramatic and daring change of career and concern.

He encountered coarse, hard-working fishermen like Peter, James, and John. They loved the lake and reveled in the fishing business. Boats and nets and wind on the water were their very life. But He called them to leave the whole business behind so that they were free to embark on other responsibilities for Him. This was not an easy rupture. Again and again they were inclined to gravitate back to the dear old fishing grounds.

To our natural minds such demands may impress us as being too drastic, too devastating. We may even feel that it is going too far for Him to ask us to alter our course in life, to sacrifice the skills and experience which mean so much to us.

The legitimate and pressing question may be asked, "Why?"

The answer is really quite simple. It is in two parts. The first is that obviously if most of our time, energy, thought, and skills are devoted to our own personal ends, they cannot be available to His highest purposes for us. Secondly, no matter how noble or fine our profession or duties may be, if accomplished by our own experience, skill, training, or industry they offer no opportunity for Christ to demonstrate what He can do in us and through us.

It is worthy of note that all through the historical record given to us of God's dealing with men and women, He often used the most unlikely people, ill-equipped and scarcely experienced at all, to achieve His greatest exploits. The basic reason He could startle the world with such ordinary people as Abraham, Joseph, Gideon, Joshua, Rahab, and Elisha was simply because their confidence did not come from their own skill or experience but from a simple, implicit faith in God Himself.

It calls for confidence in Christ to respond to His call and step out of the regular old routine. It is a ringing challenge to our faith in God to forsake the familiar life patterns of our professions or careers to step out into new fields of service for Him. It involves unshakable trust in His character that we will dare to cut off the old systems that supported us in order to do His will and accomplish His work under the guidance of His Spirit.

Part of the painful price to pay for such bold faith is the cruel taunts of our contemporaries. We will be charged with being eccentric. Some of us will be branded as fanatics. Others will be referred to as "religious kooks" out of step with the times. Even within the church there will be those who sneer at such a sacrifice.

Yet for the person brave enough to make this break with the contemporary scene of his career there are great compensations. Christ will become exceedingly precious as a constant companion. He will endow the individual with unusual capacities to carry out His wishes. He will empower the follower to accomplish tasks never dreamed of before. He will energize the disciple to impact people that otherwise would not be touched by the life of Christ.

This is because priorities have been reversed and Christ has been given supreme preeminence in the life.

Sometimes such a turnaround takes place in a simple, startling decision of the will to capitulate completely to Christ. At other times it is an ongoing process that proceeds over a period of months or years, often in fits and starts. Little by little more and more of one's time, interests, career, and enthusiasm are turned over to the Master exclusively for His use to the benefit of others as the Holy Spirit graciously guides.

One of the astonishing discoveries that attends this relinquishment of our priorities to Christ is that in many many instances the same interests and enthusiasm which bound us before are returned to us in a transmuted form. Instead of being indulged for personal self-fulfillment or self-advancement, those skills, talents, capacities, and experience are now exercised for the benefit, inspiration, and uplift of others.

We are no longer shackled into servitude to ourselves. We are set free to use all our skills to serve Christ and bring enormous blessing to our associates. What before bound us into the narrow confines of merely trying to attain our own aims and satisfy our own selfish aspirations is suddenly scattered wide, flung free from our open hands to enrich our generation. We no longer live just for our own fame or fortune, but we live to honor Christ and to promote His purposes on the planet.

We come to the conclusion that we are not our own. We do not have the right to squander our strength or our skills just on ourselves. We are now set free to pour ourselves out on behalf of others, who can now sense and know and see something of the very real life of the Living Christ made manifest in us.

As those of old used to put it so very well: "Christ has no hands in this world but mine to minister with. He has no feet but mine to carry His compassion to the needy. He has no voice but mine to speak comfort to others. He has no eyes but mine to show the love of His heart."

The layperson who determines above all things to do Christ's bidding, to come under His control, to submit wholeheartedly to the Sovereign Saviour, is inevitably placed in a position of tension between two opposite principles: that of God's will, which is to give and give and give, and that of the world's way, which is to get and get and get. Christ calls us to be generous. Society insists that we be greedy. Christ challenges us to lose our lives for others. Our culture cries out for us to save ourselves at any cost.

Some of the most sinister, yet significant, insults ever hurled at Jesus Christ during His life were the cutting, cruel taunts snarled at Him as He hung on the cross: "He saved others, He cannot save Himself!"

The phrases were much more profound than anyone ever knew on that dark and dreadful day. For if Christ had freed Himself from the nails that skewered Him to the blood-soaked cross—had He come down off that awful altar of sacrifice to save Himself—all of us would have perished in our own pollution. No, He would not, He could not—indeed, He chose deliberately not to—save Himself. Only because of His magnificent self-sacrifice has it been possible for uncounted millions to share His wondrous life across the centuries of human history.

He calls us into the same sort of sacrificial living. He challenges us to become identified with Him in bearing the burdens of the world, in sharing His sufferings in a sin-stained society. He does not offer us ease, comfort, leisure, pleasure, or self-indulgent wealth to waste upon ourselves. The way of the cross is a daily dying to the soft enticements of our comfortable culture and selfish "me" society. It is a matter of reversed priorities that are so painful to most people.

If the Christian is utterly honest, he must admit that the entire world system in which he is present is set on grasping all it can. Its ultimate aims are ease, accumulation of wealth, financial security, self-aggrandizement, social or academic prestige, and personal prominence or power in all their diverse and multifaceted forms.

The individual's energy, strength, time, attention, skills, experience, and career are all dedicated to these ends. The more he succeeds in achieving them, the more he is applauded for his accomplishments.

Standing in bold and stark contradistinction to this world view is Christ's outlook on life. He tells us to give to others, to share what we have, to bless those in need. His measure is to go the second mile even with difficult people. We are to share not only the comfortable outer coat but even the shirt off our back if need be. He asks us to extend mercy, justice, and truth even to those who want to tear us to pieces.

This is a tall order indeed. It cuts clean across all the cozy little ideas of self-interest and self-advancement advocated by our associates. And for the most part our preachers, teachers, and evangelists are either totally silent on the subject or deceive us into believing that the Master never really meant what He said.

In large part this is because they have never discovered for themselves what an adventure life can be if one truly obeys Christ and goes out to live as He did. His categorical command to us is simply this:

Seek ye first the kingdom of God [the control of Christ] and his righteousness [his right view of life] and all these things [everything necessary for life], shall be added unto you" (Matthew 6:33).

Not four percent of His followers believe or do this!

But the person prepared to lay down his or her own aims and ambitions for others, to sacrifice himself to save others, to lose his own life in finding the lost, to forsake his own fame and fortune in order to benefit his generation, to let go gladly of his career and ambitions for the good of those less fortunate—such a person will stumble over an incredible discovery: This is the way to enormous contentment in life! It is the way to find profound purpose in living, the way to find inward dignity and great honor not because of *who* we are but because of *whose* we are! We are His; we belong to Him. We are in *Christ's company*, and all is well. It is a profound paradox, but it is eternally true.

A word of explanation may help here. The self-assurance and self-worth of unregenerate men is based upon two false concepts: 1) that their capacities for learning, achieving, or influencing others are somehow self-made. The truth is that every good gift comes from God, so there is no place for human pride, which is such an affront to our Father; 2) that because human beings can project an impressive self-image on other people, even though they know themselves to be flawed within, they can also do this with Christ. But it does not work, because He knows us through and through.

Not only does He fully understand every intricacy of our genetic, hereditary makeup, but also every minute detail of the environmental influences which shaped our lives. He knows every choice made to mold the contour of our character. So He deals with us in lovely compassion, utter integrity, and complete justice. Even though knowing the worst and the best about us, He still loves us, forgives us, accepts us completely. He calls us His own!

When this awareness breaks over our souls we are set free, liberated, glad to see God as our Father, Christ as our Elder Brother, and His Spirit as our constant Companion. We are delighted to do His will. All is well within! We are bold and glad to follow Him.

Our past guilt is gone, forgiven, forgotten. Our present is glorious in His companionship. Our future is completely assured by His provisions for us. So we become people of quiet contentment in Christ. It is He who gives enormous inner dignity to our characters. We are honored to be His. And all of life becomes a genuine adventure in seeing Him achieve His supreme purposes in our lives.

Not until an individual takes Christ's teaching seriously and begins to live in quiet compliance with His straightforward commands can He, very God, be counted on to fulfill His promises. But the follower who is humbly obedient is astonished by the utter integrity of Christ. He does provide for His people in wondrous ways. He does surround them with His care. He does supply them with the vitality, energy, and enthusiasm to live on a lofty, noble plane of self-sacrifice unknown to their contemporaries.

The laity who are prepared to sacrifice their priorities and allow Christ to reverse their values will discover in actual fact that what He says is so: Whosoever shall seek to save his life shall lose it, and whosoever shall lose his life shall preserve it" (Luke 17:33).

This is the secret to abundant living in compliance with the will and wishes of Christ. The more we pour out upon others, the more He pours into our daily experience from the bounty of His own infinite supply. His presence, His power, His Person provide all we need. It is no longer "I" but rather "HE" who lives in me!

3

The Sacrifice of Possessions

The so-called "American dream" has always been one of the great driving forces in the history of our people. It has long been considered one of the fundamental rights of the residents of this continent for each person, regardless of origin or background, to become prosperous and wealthy. The old European traditions of being born into a certain class, and therefore destined to remain there, were blown away in the powerful winds of freedom that formed our societies.

It has always been regarded a profound privilege for anyone willing to work hard and apply his or her initiative to the immense natural resources of the continent to accumulate considerable private possessions. With this wealth came the power, influence, and freedom to do very much as one wished.

In all of this the acquisition of possessions assumes an all-important part of life. In actual fact, materialism has in large measure become a way of life.

Owning a home, property, all the finest furnishings, a luxury car, expensive clothes, and elegant food are considered a normal aspiration within reach of the masses. Beyond these it has also been considered appropriate to have substantial bank holdings, monetary investments, and other financial securities which form a network of security amid the ups and downs of the economic scene which is so unpredictable.

So it is not surprising that in our culture a fairly large measurement of a man and woman's "success" is in terms of their possessions. What kind of home do they own? What model car do they drive? What sort of clothes do they wear? What quality of furnishings do they buy? How flush is their financial position? Where do they go for their holidays? What scholastic credentials do they hold? And so the long list goes on in our subconscious minds.

Of course industry, business, and commerce, using all the persuasive powers of the media, coupled with high-pressure advertising, continually fuel the fires of our desires. They play upon our vanity to urge us to acquire all we can. This is the bedrock of business. We have become the most consumer-oriented society ever known. We are bedazzled by ten thousand items of trade and commerce displayed in ten thousand tantalizing ways to attract our attention and fuel our passion for possession.

In very smooth and subtle ways we become convinced that our lives really do consist in the abundance of things we possess. We are sure that the end result of our education, experience, and expertise in earning a salary are to be dedicated to the acquisition of wealth, security, and ease. We are satisfied that the supreme end of man is to be comfortable and secure amid his personal possessions.

In view of the foregoing, the vast majority of people consider it perfectly proper to have their predominant aims and ambitions in life grounded in material gain. From our earliest years, as tiny tots, we have set before us the role model of adults caught up in the feverish scramble to get ahead, to get more, to get to the top of the totem pole. Enormous thought, time, energy, and expertise are devoted to "piling it up." Because of the selfish nature of people they are seldom contented with just the first million—there must be a second, then a third. All of this becomes a grim game with no holds barred, in which people play for keeps using almost any advantage available to them, whether honest or not.

The end result has been to consider profit and advancement the bottom line in life. Little thought is given to the ethics of courtesy, decency, integrity, or generosity. These are all considered expendable in order to make a buck and gain ground.

Because this is so much a part of our culture, the Christian leaders who emerge from this milieu also consider it normal. It is not surprising that they themselves are given to precisely the same passion for possessions as their parishioners. Are we astonished to see the sort of crude preoccupation with wealth and prosperity that pervades the teaching and preaching of the more popular speakers today? Are we taken aback when huge crowds attend their seminars or buy their books which urge them to become rich and flush with financial affluence? Are we not aware that this is exactly the same philosophy of the godless world around us, and that most people just love it?

Many Christian leaders with unusual charm and glittering charisma are giving the laity a gospel of gain. Without any hint of embarrassment they entertain the masses with stirring ways to amass wealth. They are prophets who proclaim the power of profit. All of this is done by bending the Scriptures to suit their own selfish ends, using their public platforms to promote their own insidious aims and aspirations.

If in due time their devious designs are discovered, or their errors are exposed, or their outright deception is made public, they undertake to minimize the whole lie by indulging in sinister damage control. Either they blame others for being misunderstood, or they look for a scapegoat to carry away their stigma, or they simply try to bluff their way out by crying aloud that they have been wronged and victimized by their associates.

The same cover-ups, the same corruption, the same convoluted thinking so common in politics, business, or social life is carried over into the church. The basic concepts of right and wrong, love and loyalty, decency and degradation that are espoused by Christ are simply sacrificed for selfish gain and personal advantage. It is a lamentable commentary on Christianity today.

If we turn our attention to the personal life and public pronouncements of Jesus Christ we must be shocked and startled by the difference in His aims and ambitions. It is of more than passing interest that by far the greater portion of His years were spent in quiet, diligent labor as a common carpenter craftsman. There can be no doubt that He produced excellent workmanship, for He was well-known in Nazareth. He saw this work as His own proper responsibility to support His widowed mother and younger siblings. His Father above saw it too, and was well-pleased.

Quite obviously He never amassed the proceeds from His profession as a means to provide for His own ease, comfort, or wealth. He later let it be known that He did not even have a home, though foxes had dens and birds had nests. Even at the end of His short life He left no estate. He apparently owned only the common clothes of the common people—which were stripped from Him by His executioners.

Repeatedly in public He urged His hearers not to become preoccupied with such ordinary possessions as food, drink, clothing, and housing. His assurance was that anyone who put God's interests first would in fact be provided for adequately. He stated categorically that "a man's life does not consist in the abundance of things which he possesses."

When would-be disciples came to Him seeking to join His ranks and become His followers, He made the basic terms tough—at least from our soft perspective they appear that way. He told the rich young man to first go and sell all he possessed and give it to the poor, and then follow Him! He told the one with the field to forget about it. If he had set his hand to the plow there was no looking back to his possession! Always one had to count the cost of following Christ in sacrificing possessions.

Yet the modern church urges its people to be wealthy, affluent, comfortable, and cozy.

In His account of the well-to-do farmer who decided to build larger barns and increase his assets so that he could take it easy, eat, drink, and be merry, He declared the man to be an utter fool. His aims and aspirations were completely self-centered and consequently of no eternal worth to either God or others. He had established no credit with God!

These are drastic indictments, and they should sober up people whose main preoccupation is to amass possessions. On the other hand, Christ made it clear through His use of parables about the stewards and the talents entrusted to them that we are held responsible for our capacities to accumulate and manage possessions.

For Christians there are basic principles which need to be grasped if they are to use wealth wisely in the way the Master wishes.

The first of these is to recognize in genuine humility that every capacity (whether of mind, body, personality, or energy) entrusted to us for earning and accumulating possessions is a gift from God our Father. We are not self-made people, as so many suppose! Even the bounties of our natural resources are bestowed upon us in abundance by our gracious God as a generous outpouring of His provision.

It follows then that we are not little deities who in pride and pomp can parade our wealth as an indicator of prestige. Nor are we entitled to be selfish little dictators who decide entirely what we shall do with our talents, time, and assets. Rather, we are to see ourselves as humble stewards of The Most High Majesty, entrusted with His largesse, which is to be used for His honor and the benefit of His beneficiaries.

We are expected of Him to hold our responsibilities in a spirit of service to our society. He looks for us to be faithful, industrious, and honest in the discharge of our duties to both Him and our associates. We are accountable to Him for our actions.

Those who can show themselves faithful in the simple possession of small assets will soon be rewarded with ever-greater responsibilities. Many people are never entrusted with much wealth simply because they are wasteful of the little they had in the first place. Too many live on credit, deep in debt.

Whatever does come into our possession is not to be grasped and hoarded for our own selfish ends. It is appropriate and proper for us to provide adequately for our own families. We are not to be foolish in squandering what has been entrusted to our care on those who try to con us into curious schemes or false and extravagant projects. We are not to be so indulgent of others in need that we neglect to provide for our own people, and so become indebted to others for our own support. We are not to be idle and indolent even if we have the unusual capacity to earn wealth easily and quickly.

What Christ calls us to do as His followers is to be cheerful, good-willed stewards who hold whatever He has entrusted to us in open, generous hands. We are to be compassionate, warmhearted people who are ready and eager to share what we manage with others in genuine need. He told us we would always have poor people in society. The hungry, the forlorn, the lonely, the sick, and the suffering would always be a part of the human scene. To all such we are to be willing to come bearing bread and water in one hand and the good news of His Gospel, supernatural bread and water for the spirit, in the other hand.

This is how He lived. This is how He shared with others. This is how He gave what He possessed for the benefit of those around Him. He ministered as a servant to those whose lives He touched.

To live as He lived in very practical, down-to-earth terms calls for a deliberate sacrifice of some of our

111

possessions. They simply must be made totally available to His purposes upon the planet. What we give, if it is to be truly sacrificial, is much more than the mere tenth of our income, the well-known "tithe." It must far exceed what we consider the surplus over and above our legitimate needs. It must cost us something severe in personal self-sacrifice. We do not and cannot live in the lap of luxury and extravagant comfort while claiming to be sacrificing our assets for others.

To truly be able to share our possessions abundantly with those in need demands that we ourselves shall live in simplicity, doing without the finery and frills. We shall demonstrate joyous self-discipline in our own demands and desires for self-gratification. We shall be glad to do without extravagant expenditures or wasteful practices that impoverish other people.

In this way we can come to count the cost of truly following the Master in a world which for the most part urges us to live only for self-gratification. We will discover that there is deep delight in doing for others. We will find satisfaction in helping the poor and unfortunate. We will sense that our simple service is aligned with the majestic will and purpose of Christ for the planet. Caught up with Him in this work, even our most humble efforts will take on an element of dignity, honor, and adventure that is an inspiration.

As we honor Him in this way, He in turn honors us. To our constant surprise He pours into our lives and experience all that we can pour out on others. There flows from our hearts, our hands, our homes an ever-swelling stream of blessing and goodwill to others. That is the abundant life in Christ flowing out freely from us to refresh and enrich our weary old world.

4

The Sacrifice of Social Relationships

Each of us wishes to belong! A profound, powerful impulse buried deep within the human spirit constrains each of us to identify ourselves with some group in society which provides us with the sense of security, support, and sameness so essential to human happiness. In essence we are gregarious people who, though we may pride ourselves in being different in small ways, actually choose to conform to the crowd in the main concepts of life.

Were this not the case, we could not be led. It is the general willingness of human beings to conform that enables them to be marshaled and manipulated en masse by those who wield power and influence over them. There really is such a thing as the "mass mind," which if shaped to either noble or evil ends permits a people to indulge in either lofty pursuits or the most destructive practices.

In any given human society, long traditions, cultural patterns, and new ideologies continually interact to form the interwoven tapestry of human thought and conduct. Sometimes those patterns of behavior are beautiful, winsome, and uplifting. In other instances they may be brutal and savage, lacking the gracious touch of love upon the lives of the participants, who nevertheless adhere to them with tenacious fervor.

But all social relationships, whether sublime or sordid, have a compelling command over the private individual. They inevitably exert an enormous pressure upon the person to be a part of the process. And they ultimately shape his or her lifestyle. Being one of the group is so compelling that people forfeit their independence in order to become fully integrated into society. They allow not only their conduct but even their thought processes and social mores to be shaped by their own culture.

For want of a better definition we call this process "belonging to the family of man." Of course that is a very broad term which is all-embracing. In its more concise and definitive ways it can also mean belonging to a certain race, a certain country, a certain clan, a certain culture, a certain creed, a certain club, a certain church, and most importantly a certain parentage (referred to in the West as "family") in a very intimate way.

We attach enormous importance to our identity in this way. Next to our self-importance, our personal careers, and our private possessions, we consider our own social status as one of great significance. This

114

explains why people are so proud of their social relationships. It is why they are so keen to discover their "roots." It is why they love to parade their connections and strut their stuff on the stage of social life. It is why some are so ferociously loyal to their family. It is why, as a society, we speak so much about "togetherness."

Yet the startling and truly astonishing thing is that amid all of this intense dedication to our human attachments Christ comes to us and calls us into a supreme and overriding commitment to Himself. His declarations concerning our devotion to Himself more often than not cut across our family ties and social identity. To follow Him implies that a great part of the price will entail disengaging ourselves from the teachings and traditions which formerly provided us with a sense of security and support. There has to come a distinct and definite break with a culture in which we may have felt comfortable but which was at cross-purposes with His way, His truth, His life.

This may not seem too severe a cost if viewed superficially as an academic exercise. But when it is transferred into the tears and trauma and tension of fractured relationships in real life, the price is almost prohibitive for most people.

For too long, for far too long, the contemporary twentieth-century church has failed to be forthright, honest, and open in challenging its people to face the formidable call of Christ to be a "called-out" group. All through the entire history of God's dealing with the human race, the chief prerequisite for coming under His gracious care was a willingness to part ways with the world's society. His people were to be distinct, different, and set apart from their contemporaries in a definite, conspicuous allegiance to Himself.

115

Again and again the challenge rings out: "Who will be on the Lord's side?" "Choose ye this day whom you will serve!" "Why halt ye between two opinions? If the Lord be God, follow Him."

So many modern Christian leaders induce their audiences to believe that to become a Christian implies little more than merely coming into another social club. They insinuate that the cost of joining the local church really is no greater than that of joining the local service club. You simply go through the basic introductory rites, pay your fees (the week's collection), then settle in happily to be one of the boys or another of the ladies. It is as if becoming a Christian is simply another social activity added to the long list of other social relationships already enjoyed.

The astonishing truth is that Christ calls us to sacrifice any and all social relationships which in any way might diminish or deflect our undivided love and loyalty to Himself. This is a tough order indeed, and it is scarcely mentioned in most pulpits. Our leaders are terrified of telling us that many of the old and cherished attachments will have to go. They dare not declare that single-minded, strong-willed devotion to Christ will cut off our comfortable accommodation to our corrupt culture. They simply refuse to suggest that to honor Christ will cost us derision and hatred from a cynical society.

The Master was never silent on such issues. He declared openly and without apology, "If they [the society of men] have hated me, they will hate you also!" He never tried to evade the fact that it was not popular to be His follower. But He went much farther than even that. He called on those who desired to belong to His own select company to take drastic steps in disassociating themselves from the comfortable family circle which formerly supported them. Some of His statements shatter all our ideas of the sacredness of family ties and social traditions.

> Everyone that hath forsaken houses, or brethren, or sisters, or father, or mother, or wife, or children, or lands for my name's sake shall receive an hundredfold and shall inherit everlasting life. But many that are first shall be last, and the last shall be first" (Matthew 19:29,30).

This is all explosive! It is the call to drastic decisions that fracture family life and call us to tough choices at high costs. Our family ties, our domestic roots, our benign sense of belonging must all be utterly expendable. It hardly sounds like our popular preoccupation with happy "togetherness," our psychological and social formulas for finding personal fulfillment.

Because of the soft, insipid teaching so current in the church and Christian circles, many of God's people will go to almost any length to find some sort of easy accommodation with their families. They will not take a bold stand in loyalty to Christ. They are afraid of a confrontation with their culture. They fear they will alienate their children, parents, or other family members. Rather than dare to be true to Christ they softly submit to the pressure of their peers.

This really is astonishing when we pause to consider the atrocious quality of life and decadence of character so common in many Western families today. In our corrupt culture, home is no longer a haven of repose from the stresses and strains of society. Instead, the loose liaison of men and women dominated by lust and debauchery produces an appalling environment of discord and distrust in which lives and personalities are torn with sorrow and shattered with despair. Broken homes, broken hearts, and broken hopes are the seedbed from which springs so much cynicism and skepticism in our so-called smart and sophisticated society.

Christ calls us to forsake this sort of forlorn and false family association. He calls us away into a new alliance with Himself, a new allegiance to His remarkable love that is so utterly trustworthy. At times this can be a lonely life.

In our society today it is not at all uncommon for men to abandon their families. Increasingly mothers forsake their offspring. Selfish, self-indulgent young people deliberately impregnate one another, then just as willfully abort their unborn, unwanted progeny. Men seduce women while women entrap men with no intention of remaining loyal to one another. Husbands and wives cheat on one another without compunction. Couples live brazenly in common-law promiscuity that is aided and abetted by society. In an environment where no true trust prevails, youngsters are sexually abused while often only one single parent, a victim of debauchery, looks to the state for support. On every side sexual perversion feeds on pornography and social promiscuity promoted by the media.

Amid all this mayhem and madness Christ call us to be a separate, called-out people who may have to repudiate our roots. He asks that we turn from the wicked ways which have become so grossly appealing to our people and turn instead to seek His enduring love and loyalty.

This is no easy challenge in our contemporary world. For the Master calls us with a ringing call to a lofty

life of wholesomeness, holiness, and purity of thought
as well as action. He expects us to be different in a
deep and distinct dimension of definite separation
from our associates. He asks us to be willing to sacrifice sordid social relationships in order to be devoted
to His pure purposes even at the cost of isolation.

This high cost extends far beyond our own private,
immediate, flesh-and-blood families. It embraces also
the broader "family of man" as that term applies to
the whole of human society. When Christ was among
us He spoke specifically regarding the deep alienation
that would come to those who were loyal to Him. Read
carefully Matthew 10:28-42. There is scarcely a Christian family in the country today which has not known
the pain referred to on those pages. Nor has Christ
glossed over the great cost of giving our loyal allegiance to Himself!

How can it be otherwise if in fact we are determined
to do His will and set our souls to serve His purposes?
We immediately become individuals who, as He said,
are in the world (the society of man) *but not of it*. In
the darkness and decadence of our day He calls us to
be the light of His illumination. Amid the corruption
of our culture and the putrefaction of our perishing
and permissive society He calls us to be the salt of His
salvation.

Only His abundant, spontaneous, overcoming life
manifest in us as individuals can counteract all the
despair and defilement around us. It is His presence
which dispels the darkness, His power which over-
powers the pollution of our generation.

This does not mean that we disassociate ourselves
completely from our contemporaries. It does not mean
that we withdraw into cozy, safe little enclaves within
the church where our lily-white hands will never be

119

contaminated by contact with the corruption around us. It does not mean that we withdraw from the tears and trauma of our tortured world. No! A thousand times *no!*

Like Christ—empowered by His presence, constrained by His compassion, and enlivened by His overflowing life—we shall be those who in strength and loving concern reach out to lift the fallen. We shall release the prisoner bound in his own dungeon of self-depredation. We shall bring sight to the blind groping in the darkness of despair. We shall be those who bear the beauty and wonder of Christ's life and love into a wretched old world gone wrong.

When Jesus moved among us as a man, God incarnate in human form, He was scorned and scoffed at as "the friend of publicans and sinners." It was a title He rejoiced to own, for every such life that He touched He transformed. He did not hesitate to move among the lost, the lonely, the least of human beings. It was sinners He had come to call. It was lost sheep He had come to find and to save. His own character was never tarnished by contact with the defiled and despised. His own person was never polluted with picking up the perishing.

The simple reason was because of His own deep, distinct difference. He was truth in the midst of deception. He was life in the midst of death. He was light in the midst of dread human despair.

He sacrificed His own social relationship to save others.

He asks us to do the same even at the cost of being considered eccentrics by our astonished associates and fanatics by our detractors.

He stated categorically that His brothers and His sisters, even His mother, were not those of human

120

family ties but those who without hesitation did His bidding. It is thus that we are drawn into the family of God. It is in this way that we become identified with Him as our dearest Friend, and God Himself becomes our most precious parent, our Father!

5

The Sacrifice of Repentance

———

Humility is not the hallmark of our Western world. We are a proud, proud people!

A powerful haughtiness pervades our society. We parade an intellectual arrogance that is truly astonishing. We are known the world over for our abrasive attitude of superiority. Even in spiritual matters we often behave as though we are a cut above other cultures.

All the traditional arguments advanced to support our so-called superior lifestyle are well-known. We have been taught from infancy that we possess the finest political system ever devised for man. Under it we claim to enjoy the privileges of freedom, liberty, and equality to live as we wish, never before bestowed

123

on human society, even though our own society is so corrupt.

In the realm of science and technology we boast of our accomplishments, research, and discovery as though the intelligence for all such advances reposed in our halls of human study and not in the wisdom bestowed on man by God our Father. Our academic arrogance is beyond belief. Our ultimate confidence is in the scientific process.

We pride ourselves upon our intellectual standards. We are sure our educational systems provide the most sophisticated enlightenment ever known, even though rank cynicism and unrelieved despair are the end product of our human philosophies.

There is no end to our boasting about having the highest standard of living in the world, even though it is maintained by incredible waste of our natural resources and an irreversible pollution of the environment. We seem to insist that paved highways, flashing multitudes of cars, elaborate homes, fine furniture, and dazzling clothes denote the ultimate in attainment.

We are sure that our social network of services eclipses anything ever before known in human history—this despite the fact that many who serve society in this way are themselves derelict, incapable of providing answers to the agony of our age.

And in Christian endeavors, whatever form they take, we parade our programs and projects as though they were of superior spiritual quality. We have deluded ourselves into believing that our scientific skills, modern technology, and high-powered business methods, if applied to the church, can usher in the kingdom of God on a grand worldwide scale. The proud shout of the twentieth-century church is to reach the whole world for Christ in our generation. It is always assumed that this will be accomplished by means of mass communication: literature, radio, television, films, records, aircraft, satellites, and computer technology.

All of the above somehow excite us tremendously. With our materialistic mind-set we quickly get caught up in any movement of this magnitude. We assume rather naively that, given enough money, men, and skilled management, we can make any mission a success. So we call great conventions, assemble huge sums of financial support, set out special so-called spiritual strategies, and then go out to accomplish our aims in the world, assuming that the projects will astonish everyone.

All of this panders precisely to those aspects of our individual lives which were discussed in the preceding chapters. Because of our backgrounds we find it compelling to cater to our own selfish self-interests. Here we can promote our own careers and advance our own interests. Grandiose church schemes can be a display for wealth, power, and influence because of our affluence. And in all this we find fertile ground in which to cultivate our social relationships and parade our personal contacts with celebrities.

In the face of all this excitement it is sobering to hear Christ tell us that the kingdom of God is really not of such human design at all. It is not an outward demonstration of power, influence, or strategy displayed in tangible terms that are measured by our five fallible senses. Rather, He states categorically that it is the secret inner process of spiritual reorientation which goes on within a human soul that has received Him as the Most High Majesty.

The absolute bedrock requirement needed for this to happen is a simplicity of spirit and humility of heart akin to that of a small child. Jesus actually picked up a tiny tot one day, held the youngster snugly in His strong arms, and declared without apology:

> I say unto you, Except ye be converted and become as little children, ye shall not enter into the kingdom of heaven. Whosoever therefore shall humble himself as this little child, the same is greatest in the kingdom of heaven (Matthew 18:3,4).

In our Western world we simply do not want to talk about humility. We are self-centered people who are proud of our professions, proud of our achievements, proud of our possessions, proud of even our spiritual stature. Millions of modern Christians boast of their special church affiliation. They are urged to parade their special spiritual gifts. They flaunt their Biblical knowledge and pose as somewhat superspiritual individuals in society.

It is not surprising that all of this is an affront to God our Father. He simply is not impressed. As ever of old, He looks for men and women broken in spirit and contrite in heart (will) who seek Him in utter penitence. It is with such souls that He delights to reside. But this will never happen unless there is genuine repentance from pride, profound remorse for our perverseness, and relinquishment of our sordid pollution.

When John the Baptist, the greatest man born of a woman, came as Christ's forerunner he preached the absolute need for repentance. When Christ started out on His public ministry He called for repentance.

126

When the apostles of the early church arrested the attention of their society they demanded repentance. Yet the Christian leaders of our generation are almost silent on the subject. They are reluctant to carry out Christ's clear command that repentance and remission of sins should be preached in His name among all the nations of the earth. Read Luke 24:45-48.

The question needs to be asked clearly and very emphatically: "What is repentance from God's viewpoint? What does it demand of man?"

It is absolutely essential for laypeople to understand this. If there is to be harmony, unity, and goodwill between the Living Christ and us common men and women, it must be based not only on the majestic accomplished work of Christ but also on our personal willingness to repent of our pride, our perverseness, and our pollution.

In essence repentance is a disclosure to us of our undone condition before the absolute love, purity, justice, and incandescent righteousness of the Risen Christ. It is borne in upon our stained souls so smeared with selfishness, our spirits so sullied with pride, our daily behavior so corrupted with evil that we are at odds with God our Father. *We actually become very acutely aware that we have set ourselves up in antagonism to Him.* We are at enmity with God. We are rebels living in open defiance of His best intentions for us. We have set ourselves up in pride as supreme in our own affairs. So we refuse to receive Him as Monarch in our lives. We close Him out of our considerations. We live as though He were dead.

The actual truth is just the opposite: He declares us to be dead in our sins and iniquities, needing desperately to cast ourselves upon His mercy in profound

127

repentance and beseeching Him to impart His divine and eternal life to us.

Repentance, if it is genuine, arises from a deep and profound conviction by Christ's Spirit that we are indeed wrongdoers who in sinister sin against Him have become alienated from Him. Though in His wondrous grace, generosity, and love He extends to us His mercy, forgiveness, and acceptance on the basis of His own magnanimous self-sacrifice, He demands that we for our part turn from our wicked ways, repent of our wrongs, seek His companionship, and claim His amazing justification through total forgiveness.

Repentance is not a once-for-all experience that takes place only at the time of initial conversion. It is in fact a daily sacrifice in which we see ourselves as we really are in the white, intense light of Christ's character and His Word, so that we need to turn to Him for cleansing and for forgiveness. It is the continual repudiation of evil in our lives. It is the humble admission of having missed the mark in the high calling to which Christ calls us. It is the bold willingness to face our sins and to come to hate them with utter disdain and stern intensity because they are such a grief to Christ and such a corruption of our own characters.

In godly repentance there is a profound personal sorrow for the suffering which our sins bring to our fondest friend, Jesus Christ. There is genuine remorse for the pain and sadness that our wrong attitudes and rotten behavior bring to others around us. There is horrendous self-humiliation because we know full well that we are not living our best. Our misconduct, our selfishness, our pride, our pollution corrode our own characters and contaminate our own conduct.

Such repentance drives us to our knees. It starts our tears. It wrings the desperate inner cry of the spirit from us: "O God in Christ, be merciful to me a sinner!"

When we examine the Biblical record of God dealing with men who walked with Him in close communion, it is remarkable to discover how they were driven to repentance: righteous Job of old; David, a monarch after God's own heart; Isaiah, the great prophet; Peter, the flaming apostle. All were individuals who, when they saw with inner clarity their own undone condition, were stricken with acute remorse and cried out in repentance for restoration.

In our own age, every great spiritual awakening that has occurred anywhere in the world has been marked with genuine repentance. In response to the entreaty of God's people for renewal of supernatural work in their midst, Christ has come by His own Spirit to perform a sovereign work of conviction among Christians and non-Christians. No longer must people be persuaded that they are in need of salvation. Instead they are made acutely aware that they stand undone in the overwhelming presence of The Holy One. In deep contrition they humble themselves before His Person and cry out in earnestness for His mercy, His cleansing, His pardon, His acceptance.

Having done this, they know assuredly that their sins and iniquities are not only utterly abhorrent to Christ but are the pollution which separates them from Him. They must not only accept His pardon and claim His wondrous forgiveness but turn away entirely from their wicked ways. For to repent means not only to turn and seek Christ's acceptance but also to turn deliberately from wrongdoing. It means to quit sinning at any cost. It means that one refuses to disobey Christ and so crucify Him again.

There is a formidable price to pay in all of this. That price is to forgo all the vain enticements of the social scene that pander to our pride while we walk with Christ in humility of heart.

The world with all its self-deception and facetious cynicism will scoff at anyone who chooses to follow Christ in contrition of spirit. They will laugh loud and long at the person who sets himself to do Christ's bidding in lowliness of mind. They will demean the man or woman brave enough to part ways with the crowd in humble service and loving loyalty to His Majesty, the Lord Jesus Christ. They will ostracize the individual who above all else, in genuine repentance, comes under the control of Christ, allowing Him to establish His kingdom within their soul.

To the world—so proud, so perverse, so polluted— the life of purity, uprightness, integrity, justice, and mercy to which Christ calls us is all utterly impractical and an irritation. It simply does not make sense to men and women who despise righteousness and revel in iniquity. They call good evil and evil they laughingly call good.

For the true child of God, called of Christ into His companionship, introduced into the family of the Father, and sealed by God's Spirit into a new citizenship in a new kingdom from above, the world system becomes foreign territory. We no longer feel at home or at ease in the contemporary scene. This world is now no longer our permanent residence. We discern in a profound and powerful way that we have altered our allegiance by giving it to Christ and His eternal kingdom. We have assumed the status of strangers, nonresident aliens, pilgrims passing through the shifting scenes of our ever-changing, skeptical society.

Here there is nothing stable, nothing sure, nothing secure.

We have found a brand-new center for life, and that center is Christ. It is Him whom we love above all else with unswerving loyalty. It is Him whom we serve in unflinching faith.

The world will call us mad eccentrics. He will call us His own precious people!

6

The Sacrifice of Obedience in Love and Loyalty

It is well-known that we live in a permissive age. What is not so well-known is the dire consequence of such a mind-set for the Christian. It immediately brings about formidable inner struggles within the soul. It prevents the person who wishes to give whole-hearted allegiance to Christ from doing so. It challenges His claim to our love and loyalty. It can, if allowed to do so, render us well nigh impotent in our walk with Him.

It will help to understand this great danger if we examine its basic human philosophy. In a permissive society the rights of the individual are considered to be above those of the society as a whole. The person's private conduct is said to be almost sacrosanct. He or

133

she is permitted to do even the most despicable things without accountability to others. All sorts of legal mechanisms are put in place to protect the so-called civil liberties of the individual, even though his or her conduct be most unethical or even immoral and destructive to others.

Put in the plainest possible terms, what this really means is that no one feels constrained to come under authority. Children feel no compunction to obey their parents, their teachers, or anyone else. The parents in turn feel no profound need to be accountable to their employers, their superiors in any given social setting, or even to the state. The idea of obedience to others or submission to authority of any kind becomes passé.

In interpersonal relationships, all sense of noble and ethical behavior is eroded away. Men and women discard the traditional values of courtesy, integrity, commitment, and decency. In the broader realm of social mores there is decreasing respect for law and order. More and more people openly defy all authority. So society, our much-vaunted civilization, teeters on the edge of anarchy.

There is perhaps no other single aspect of our twentieth-century Western world which poses such an enormous peril for us as a people. It is this insidious corrosion which brings about so much distrust and anxiety. If each individual behaves as if he or she has no other personal responsibility to either God or man, the end result is mayhem and madness. This thought pattern has become deeply entrenched among us. It blatantly blocks out the profound and lofty concepts of deep loyalty and genuine love which otherwise can make life lovely and secure.

As was explained in an earlier chapter, the root cause of this calamity is pride. But beyond this there lies the broader realm of genuine love and loyalty to others, both God and man. Though the modern church has spoken endlessly about God's love for man, many of our leaders have been strangely silent about man's obligation to love God, to love others, and to demonstrate this love with undeviating loyalty.

The reason for this remarkable reticence is simply that the claims of Christ upon His followers in this area are very demanding. He was utterly adamant in stating that the first and greatest commandment was to love God with all of our beings and the second was to love others as ourselves. This love of which He spoke so freely and so often was not some sort of soft, sentimental affection. Rather, it was the terribly tough self-discipline of doing His bidding at any cost, of laying down our own lives for the sake of others, of submitting gladly to the wishes and will of God our Father.

This is precisely how Christ Himself lived. It was the essence of His relationship to His Father and to others. He stated unashamedly that He had not come to do His own will. His very meat and drink and life were to do His Father's will. His very words and statements were His Father's. His work was His Father's work. He was under authority. His whole life experience was that of one under command, fulfilling completely every detail of divine law and order.

None of this sits very comfortably with contemporary man. The whole idea that Christians are to be a people under divine authority, subject implicitly to Christ's control and obedient to His commandments, repels most people both inside the church and outside of it. The cost of giving Christ the sacred sacrifice of our total, wholehearted obedience is too prohibitive! The predators in our pulpits prefer to have us believe

135

that He really did not mean what He said. They deliberately dilute His demands and delude their followers into believing that one can live a split life of divided love and divided loyalties. With one half we serve our own self-interests and adhere to our social concept of personal independence; with the other half we begrudgingly and reluctantly serve Christ and others.

Jesus Christ stated emphatically that one could not live this way; a person cannot serve two masters. Either you hate the one and love the other or vice versa. It must be one or the other. To try to do both is to ride two horses moving in opposite directions, only to fall between the two in utter failure and frustration. This explains the sad futility of so many Christians. It is why they are so impotent, so ineffective, so compromised.

Some Christian leaders, who themselves have never come under authority to Christ, complain that to do so is to be bound into legalism. They contend that to be subject to the commands of Christ is to be brought into rigid ritualism of some sort that demeans the individual. They insist that one should be set free from any sort of restraints, even if it abuses Christ and panders to our old self-life.

What they fail to realize is that every commandment, law, precept, or principle established by God is for our well-being. His wishes and will are not repressive regulations intended to demean us or diminish our enjoyment of life. Quite the opposite—they are the definitive guidelines which, if we obey them, guarantee our ultimate welfare. They are of divine design to insure us of an abundant life. They release us from bondage to self and to sin. They set us free into the paths of right living in following Christ. They are light to our feet amid the darkness. They are an expression of His love that dispels our despair on the path of our pilgrimage with Him.

As we choose decisively each day to comply with His commands in wholehearted obedience, we discover His presence, His love, His life engulfing us. Why? Because He delights to give His Spirit to the person who obeys Him (Acts 5:32). He cannot do this for the one in open rebellion to Him, nor even for the one who quietly resents His authority.

A careful, prayerful study of all that Christ said in His last discourse with His disciples just before His death reveals a remarkable truth. Simply stated, it is this: *The only proof positive that we truly love Him and are loyal to Him lies in our willingness to come under His control and comply with His commands.* The person who does this daily in single-minded devotion is the individual with whom Christ delights to dwell. This is the ultimate secret to having Him share all of life with us. Read carefully John chapters 14, 15, 16, and 17.

This is in essence the sacrifice of glad obedience.

It demonstrates to Him and to others our genuine love for God. It is the empirical evidence of our unswerving loyalty. It is offered gladly and joyously. Why? We love Him because He loved us in the first place. *His love is being returned to Him.*

It may very well be asked, "How is this done in a very practical, effective manner?" After all, it is one thing to be told what we should do and quite another to obey Christ in daily interaction.

First of all it takes the self-discipline of time. It is absolutely essential to sacrifice a segment of each day for an attentive reading and meditation over His Word. This segment of the day is a special interlude during which we actually meet with Him in quiet attentiveness, open and receptive to His Spirit, who in a quiet and profound manner impresses upon us new and fresh insights into Christ's character and desires.

It is most helpful to begin by reading through one of the Gospel records of Christ's own life. Take a notebook in hand and write the explicit instructions given there one by one, each at the top of a new page. Each new day meditate over what He said to do. Read other passages bearing on this theme. Ask for a clear and explicit spiritual understanding of what His intentions are for you.

Then in your own handwriting state clearly, in precise layman's language, below the page heading, precisely what He is asking you to do. It may take you several days or weeks of deliberate prayer and searching to find out for sure what to write. Having done this, bow yourself humbly before Christ and give Him your assurance that you will diligently *do His bidding* on that point. You will undertake to actually carry out His wishes and comply with His will in this specific area of life.

It may very well take as long as two full years to work your way diligently through a book like Matthew. But you will never be the same person again. In the process, if you are honest before God, His Word will transform you.

Secondly, one must set his will to go out and without dispute or debate actually carry out Christ's commands in the midst of life. It is not enough to know His will, to think about it, or even to discuss it. *It must be done, no matter what the personal cost.* This may involve intense suffering of self-humiliation, self-embarrassment, or ridicule from others.

Here is an example. Christ says clearly, "Love your enemies, bless them that curse you, do good to them that hate you, and pray for them which despitefully use you and persecute you!" What a tall order for anyone to take seriously!

This involves going to those who detest us and apologizing for our own rotten attitudes toward them. It calls for us to care about them enough that we not only extend compassion and goodwill to them but also go the second mile in extending total forgiveness to them for all their wrongs and abuse. Beyond this we actually, earnestly pray for their welfare and bestow on them any personal blessings we can.

None of this is easy. It is not natural. It calls for enormous personal sacrifice of ourselves. It will often entail acute suffering because even our best intentions and finest motives will be viewed with deep skepticism and perhaps even be scoffed at.

So it can be seen that Christ's challenge for us to carry out His commands is not something soft or sweet or sentimental. It calls for the sacrifice of implicit obedience, which often means paying a formidable personal price of humiliation and suffering.

Put in very simple, practical terms, this is the true meaning of "taking up the cross of Christ daily in life." It means that the great central I (ego) in my life is crossed out as I submit myself to His will. His desires override my will. And I am crucified with Him so He can fully live out His life in me.

For the average layperson this whole process as a way of life may seem to be utterly prohibitive and quite beyond his or her ability to undertake. However, there is great good cheer that is not often understood which accompanies such a life of self-sacrifice. It is this: Only in this way do you ever come to fully know

God in Christ. It is in this manner, as you choose to deliberately lay down your life daily for Him and for others, that you discover the stimulating surge of His presence—His very life, His love, His Spirit, His energy and strength—surging into your spirit, into your soul, into your very body. He does in fact become your life! It is no longer *you* but *Christ living in you* that enables you to move and live and have your very being in quiet obedience to His will.

Only in this way (His way) do you come to know firsthand the essential character of the Risen Christ. He becomes your closest confidant. He is your dearest associate. He is the motivation and inspiration for your very life. He is your life itself, as He Himself said so plainly: "He that abideth in me, and I in him, the same bringeth forth much fruit; for without me ye can do nothing!" (John 15:5).

When the Christian's life becomes of this caliber, then the cost of following Christ is no longer beyond our ability to consider. Rather, by degrees we begin to discover that it can actually become a positive delight to do His bidding. Our walk with Him becomes an adventure in living as He daily demonstrates to us His capacity to overcome the world through His amazing faith imparted to us.

We no longer live for ourselves. Instead, we go out positively with quiet assurance to serve others and bless our generation in His great name. We begin to live by implicit faith in Christ, who calls us and gives Himself to us daily.

7

The Sacrifice of Faithful Service

In our busy and very boisterous world of the late twentieth century a certain tough and callous quality has crept into all of life. People are not as courteous or considerate of each other as they once were. Politeness and gracious behavior are less apparent. The gentle greeting and genuine desire to be of service to others is much forgotten.

Because of this, it is not uncommon to hear people ask such simple yet searching questions as "Whatever happened to service?" or "Where have good manners gone?" or "Where do we find old-fashioned faithfulness to duty?"

Even secular magazines, worldly editorial boards, and hard-shelled publishers are puzzled by the phenomenon. They devote pages and pages of their periodicals to such themes as "What happened to ethics?" or "Where does one find service?"

All of this seems ironical in a society where we boast blatantly that the fastest-growing segment of our economy lies in the so-called service industries. In fact the rapid emergence of service-supply companies and their affiliates is regarded by some to be an industrial revolution surpassing that of the mechanical era of the past hundred years.

In the midst of this immense upheaval, service as such is not something offered as a gesture of goodwill and generosity for the well-being of the recipient. Quite the opposite! It is offered as a commercial commodity that must be paid for in hard cash. A classic illustration which any of us can easily understand is the so-called "service" station. Either you pump your own gas, clean your own windows, and check your own oil *or you pay some reluctant attendant to do the job.*

This peculiar philosophy of life has spilled over into every segment of society. It is not restricted to just the city streets of giant metropolitan communities or the tough environment of huge industrial complexes. It has crept into the general thinking and public attitudes of all our people. So-called public servants withhold the services they are paid to supply. Doctors, nurses, teachers, firemen, and even policemen do not hesitate to withhold service in order to obtain certain benefits and higher pay.

Nor has Christian service to the community remained unscathed. Some of us are utterly astonished at the secular demands made by those in church leadership or other associated fields of service. The salaries they command, the benefits they demand, the life-style they insist upon, and the security they expect are equivalent to anything found in the world.

Men and women who claim to have been called into some sort of special Christian service, even missionaries, require advance assurance that their support will be met, that every possible exigency in the enterprise will be covered, that their work will be handsomely rewarded, and that at any moment they feel constrained to return to the secular field, they are free to do so.

All of this is a far cry from the sort of service to which Christ called His associates. It was pointed out in the very first chapter of this book that He made it abundantly clear that He came to minister (serve) and not to be ministered to by others. His purpose upon the planet as God in human form was not to get and get and get but to give and give and give.

When He sent out His own followers on their first mission forays, His instructions were explicitly clear. They can be read very readily in Matthew 10:5-42. But central to all His explicit commands was this theme: "FREELY YE HAVE RECEIVED, FREELY GIVE!"

From Christ's perspective the daily sacrifice of one's service to others was and is an integral part of life. To lay one's life down for the benefit and well-being of those who might benefit by such a sacrifice was an accepted part of paying the price to be one of His people. The cost, the personal cost, for such personal service to the society of men can be very high, very demanding, very humbling, very painful.

The reasons for this are not always obvious. Too often the church and Christian leaders mislead the laity into believing that there is something heroic, romantic, spectacular, or even exciting about service for Christ. Much more often simple service to our suffering world in Christ's name is pretty drab, very unexciting, replete with sorrow, touched by suffering, and even spurned. Odd as it may seem, the giving of one's very life—of his time, of his strength, of his skill—may not even be appreciated or acknowledged by the recipients. This is why the service, the compassion, the love, the devotion must in essence be given to Christ Himself in an outpouring of our devotion to Him.

He made this very plain for us to understand. His own life was a shining example of generous, gracious, selfless service to His society. He did nothing but good for others. Yet He received remarkably little gratitude from His generation. In due course He was crucified by His contemporaries even though He had benefited thousands and thousands in His time. It all seems incongruous, but it is a clear demonstration to us of the fickle, unpredictable quality of human nature and human conduct.

He told us that even if we give a cup of cold water to assuage another's thirst we should see it as an act of compassionate service to Himself. We live to please Him. We dare not even hope for appreciation from our associates.

All of this might seem exceedingly difficult for us to do if we only see ourselves as mere servants. But in reality we are much more than that in Christ's view. We are His "friends." He actually calls us by this compelling name. We are friends caught up with Him in the common cause of enormous compassion for a perishing world. So to be His co-workers, co-laborers, and co-givers lends a whole new impetus to our service.

But beyond even this beautiful association He sees us as His brothers and His sisters in the family of God. We actually are the sons and daughters of our Father. We are heirs and joint heirs with Jesus Christ. We are bound together in wondrous bonds, not of slavery but of sonship. So we see our service not as a duty but as a royal privilege bestowed upon us by His Majesty. Just as the monarchy of the Royal Family is established to serve its people, so we are given the royal responsibility to serve our generation in faith and goodwill.

The motivation and inspiration for our service, no matter how drab, mundane, or lowly it may be, does not come from our compassion to our community. It comes instead from a deep devotion to Christ, an unshakable confidence that He can sustain us in any situation, an unflinching faith in His unfailing faithfulness to us no matter how tough the task He calls us to accept.

Ultimately all or anything that we accomplish in quiet service is because of Him: "It is God who worketh in us, both to will and to do of his good pleasure!" It is Christ who by His Spirit sheds abroad in us His own supernatural love and enables us to love others as He does. It is Christ who by His presence provides us with His strength to stand up to the strain of His service. It is Christ who by His daily encouragement enables us to face formidable odds in quiet faith and thereby overcome the world around us.

Without such simple, unpretentious faith in Christ it is impossible to either please God or truly benefit man. Without the adventure of seeing our Father doing wondrous things on our behalf amid the drudgery of our daily duties, the best of service can become a bore. It is the supernatural element of His wondrous intervention in our simple service that injects an extraordinary dimension of delight into our work with Him. The most ordinary and mundane round of responsibility can be ignited and set alight by His presence with us and His part in making it a noble endeavor.

It is this dimension of divine participation in our daily activities that can make our service to Christ and to our community an adventure. We are astonished at what He can achieve through our little lives. We are humbled at how He can touch a thousand hearts and heal a hundred homes because we trust Him quietly to do what we cannot do ourselves.

If we will but gladly, freely, joyously put all we are and own at His disposal He will take all we offer and bless it, use it, and distribute it to the needy to the ends of earth. He took a small lad's sardines and buns. He blessed them, shared them, and fed ten thousand hungry people. He can do as much and more for anyone prepared to give Him what they have in glad abandon.

Our service as God's people should never bear the earmark of self-serving interest so common in our culture. For example, we speak of people "serving" on boards, committees, or other social functions. Far too often these positions carry with them the prestige and prominence which pander to pride and social status. If carried out in humility of heart, such service is fine. If done for public applause, it is of no value at all. We need the servant mind of Christ in all we do.

For the Christian who truly knows Christ and revels in His constant companionship there simply are no distinctions between so-called "secular service" and "sacred service." There are no boundary lines between "full-time Christian ministry," as some call it, and the role of the common laity who love God and minister with unfailing loyalty to Christ in all they do.

All of life becomes a sacrament for the person whose very being is centered in the Living Christ and in whom God has opportunity to demonstrate something of His own character and conduct to a watching world. Such a life of service will bear the imprint of the Master upon it. Whatever labor of love is done, no matter how ordinary or mundane, will be undertaken to please Christ, to honor His reputation at stake in us, and to enrich, uplift, and benefit others.

Any service offered by a Christian should be notable for its high quality. The work should be well done, with integrity and thoroughness. We should not do a shoddy job. The service should be provided punctually and in keeping with our personal commitments to others. Work only half-done and delivered late with lame excuses is not acceptable for a servant of His Majesty. Lastly, our service for Christ is not given grudgingly or under duress. Rather, it is offered daily as a sacrifice of praise and goodwill to Him who loves us. It spills out from us as a fragrance of good cheer and inspiration to those whose lives we touch in this ordinary way.

The Christian whose daily deportment is of this caliber is the one who will very soon be asked, "What makes you so different?" This is the individual who can then calmly and quietly share the great good news of our Father's love with those around him, because he is living a life that is well-pleasing to God and that blesses others.

The other beautiful aspect of such service is that it provides our Father with a lovely opportunity to demonstrate His remarkable faithfulness to His servant. Like small children, we trust Him confidently to lead us gently in all we do. We turn to Him for wisdom and skill in all our service. We draw from Him the strength and stamina to serve faithfully even under the most adverse circumstances. We rely upon Him to supply the good cheer, buoyancy and goodwill to live noble lives in any setting. Our implicit faith is in Him for all we need, whether for body, soul, or spirit.

Few Christians in the contemporary scene live this way. Most of them live exactly the same way their worldly associates do. They rely on their own skills. They depend on human resources. They turn to human technology for guidance. They live by the basic data available to them through their five fallible senses. They do not live by a vibrant, shining faith in Christ. Consequently He is given little opportunity to ever reveal Himself in all His wonder to a skeptical society.

But for the person prepared to walk with Christ in close communion, living humbly with Him in unflinching faith, all of life can become a benediction. It matters not what form or shape our service may be— dusting furniture, washing clothes, pulling weeds, visiting a friend, greeting strangers with a smile, teaching a class, serving a meal, preparing a lecture, writing a letter, writing a book that will touch ten thousand lives—each can be done as a superb service to our Lord and as a blessing to our generation.

Only as our lives reflect the very character of Christ, the Glory of God, will they serve as a daily sacrifice that is well-pleasing to Him. He told us, "He that hath seen me hath seen the Father!" Exactly the same can be true of us today. In this way Christ is honored as men get a glimpse of God in His children.

Afterword

Anyone who has read this book is bound to wonder about the background and firsthand experience of the author. From what perspective does he write? What gives him ground for the statements made? Those are appropriate questions to pose.

Here is a very brief overview of my lifelong interest in and involvement with Christian endeavors.

I was born and raised in the midst of a splendid mission enterprise in East Africa. My parents were laypeople of enormous devotion both to Christ and to the Africans. Under their loving, humble leadership a strong enduring church of great vitality was established. This I witnessed firsthand as a growing youth, astonished at what Christ could accomplish in such a sordid society with simple people.

Afterword

During the subsequent years of early manhood my studies, career, and assignments introduced me to almost every denomination in Christendom. Through wide contacts with all sorts of churches around the world I became acquainted not only with their basic beliefs but also with the thrust of their leadership. It has been my honor to observe firsthand the work of Christ's servants in some 30 different countries. These endeavors range from the most basic pioneer works among primitive people to the very sophisticated projects undertaken in great metropolitan centers.

In all of this I too have been on the pilgrim path, endeavoring to walk ever more closely with Christ. His call has come to me just as clearly as it did to the disciples of His day. In my own private relationship to the Living Christ each of the challenges set out in this book have had to be met in a positive, personal response. This is not a theoretical treatise based on what others think or profess; it is the distilled essence of my own quiet walk with God across the long years of my life. Sometimes the path was painful.

Gradually and gently Christ by His gracious Spirit called me into ever-wider fields of service to His people. Because I had seen firsthand, behind the scenes, so much that dismayed me in various Christian endeavors I was not keen to go, especially late in life. Still, the loving perseverance of Christ prevailed upon my reluctant soul. At last complete capitulation to His will became my lodestar in life.

Steadily and surely He led me to speak and work for Him as a common layperson. All sorts of people in all sorts of places, much to my surprise, asked me to come and speak to them about Christ. Many begged me to put into book form the basic truths shared with them in simplicity. The intense hunger that some had to truly know and love Christ moved me deeply.

As time went on I was invited to start Bible studies. Some of these were held in homes, some in country clubs, some in churches. The sessions were wide open to anyone in the community who cared to come. People were drawn into these groups from every sort of background. They shared with me openly about the great concern they felt for the lack of leadership in their own churches. This became one of the ever-recurring themes across the years. They felt deprived and misled by those who were in their pulpits or leadership roles.

In all of this it became increasingly clear to me that there was a drastic need for bold people to come forward who would confront the corruption of our culture in the name of Christ. The modern church was being seduced by our sordid society, and in fact we faced a great peril from predators in our pulpits.

Eventually, in wondrous ways of His own design, Christ provided unusual opportunities for me to speak to groups of pastors and outstanding lay Christians active in leadership. Again these people came from a wide diversity of denominations.

Many of these dear men and women have spoken to me privately about their great anguish over God's work. They have shared their tears and their triumphs with me. Most important, they have told me of their burning concern for Christ's church in this century. So both the laity and some of their leaders have urged me to write this book.

The simple, final conclusion to which I have come is that only Christ Himself is the One who must be lifted up to lead us. Ultimately it is His call that counts. It is

His character and His commitments to us that validate our faith. It is His very life active and at work within us which alone can make us triumph in His might.

That is why in this book Christ has always been held up in full view for everyone to see. He is always looked to as the final reference in our responsibilities. He is the One who can take us, despite our limitations, and accomplish His great purposes on the planet. He is our precious Friend, yet also the Most High Majesty who in wondrous ways designs to share our days with us in joyous delight.

He is our Great Good Shepherd.
In His presence all is well.
He is here! Bless His name!
Let us respond humbly and gladly to
   His call,
      "FOLLOW ME!"

Other Good Harvest House Reading

THE SEDUCTION OF CHRISTIANITY—Spiritual Discernment in the Last Days
by *Dave Hunt* and *T.A. McMahon*

Since its release in August 1985, *The Seduction of Christianity* has become one of the most talked about books in Christian circles. Examining dangerous and extrabiblical practices that are influencing millions, Christians need to become aware of fake doctrine so they won't fall prey to the seduction of Christianity.

BEYOND SEDUCTION—A Return to Biblical Christianity
by *Dave Hunt*

Beyond Seduction calls believers back to the true biblical foundations of Christianity and God's promise of abundant life. In *Beyond Seduction* author/researcher Dave Hunt thoroughly explores the biblical and historical view of Christian teachings within the church, including meditation, the proper view of self, faith, divine revelation, prayer, healing, and psychological teachings. This provocative new book will help readers to build their faith and dependence upon God alone.

A CALL TO DISCERNMENT
Distinguishing Truth from Error in the Contemporary Church by *Jay E. Adams*

Many Christians are confused by recent scandals involving noted Christian personalities. They are wondering how to evaluate what is from God and what is simply the invention of man. Dr. Jay Adams, noted biblical counselor and author of more than 50 books, has written a much-needed examination of the subject of spiritual discernment. He outlines step by step how anyone can take a teaching by any preacher or Bible teacher and examine the Scriptures to discern whether that statement accurately reflects God's Word.

WHATEVER HAPPENED TO ORDINARY CHRISTIANS?
by *Jim Smoke*

For the first time in history, we have created our very own Christian "Star System," elevating and imitating those people with extraordinary accomplishments. This has placed tremendous pressure on every committed believer to be a superstar in his or her Christian performance and has diminished the importance of living the simple and obedient Christian life.

> What does it mean to be a successful Christian according to biblical standards?
>
> How can the Christian's life be pleasing to God in our fast-paced, materialistic society?

You will find tremendous encouragement as noted author Jim Smoke explains how.

THE BIBLICAL VIEW OF SELF-ESTEEM
by *Jay Adams*

The powerful and influential humanistic message has subtly permeated the church under the guise of "self-esteem," "self-worth," and "self-love." Dr. Jay Adams, renowned biblical counselor and noted author, evaluates the self-esteem movement and offers a truly biblical view of self.

THE NAKED CHURCH
by *Wayne Jacobsen*

Clothed in expensive architecture, elaborate programs, and impressive statistics, the modern church has all too often traded the presence of God for the nakedness of religious form. Jacobsen gives a clear and inspiring view of what true intimacy with God entails and offers a blueprint that every person can use to build that intimacy.

Dear Reader:

We would appreciate hearing from you regarding this Harvest House nonfiction book. It will enable us to continue to give you the best in Christian publishing.

1. What most influenced you to purchase *Predators in Our Pulpits*?
   ☐ Author   ☐ Recommendations
   ☐ Subject matter   ☐ Cover/Title
   ☐ Backcover copy   ☐ _____

2. Where did you purchase this book?
   ☐ Christian bookstore ☐ Grocery store
   ☐ General bookstore   ☐ Other
   ☐ Department store

3. Your overall rating of this book:
   ☐ Excellent ☐ Very good ☐ Good ☐ Fair ☐ Poor

4. How likely would you be to purchase other books by this author?
   ☐ Very likely   ☐ Not very likely
   ☐ Somewhat likely   ☐ Not at all

5. What types of books most interest you?
   (check all that apply)
   ☐ Women's Books   ☐ Fiction
   ☐ Marriage Books   ☐ Biographies
   ☐ Current Issues   ☐ Children's Books
   ☐ Self Help/Psychology ☐ Youth Books
   ☐ Bible Studies   ☐ Other _____

6. Please check the box next to your age group.
   ☐ Under 18   ☐ 25-34   ☐ 45-54
   ☐ 18-24   ☐ 35-44   ☐ 55 and over

Mail to: Editorial Director
Harvest House Publishers
1075 Arrowsmith
Eugene, OR 97402

Name _____

Address _____

City _____ State _____ Zip _____

Thank you for helping us to help you in future publications!